BUSINESS REPORT WRITING

COLLEGE EDITION

by

Burton L. Fischman, B.S., M.A., Ph.D.
Associate Professor of English
Bryant College, Smithfield, Rhode Island

P.A.R. Incorporated ● **Abbott Park Place** ● **Providence, Rhode Island 02903**

BUSINESS REPORT WRITING

College Edition

Printed in the United States of America

Library of Congress Cataloging in Publication Data

Fischman, Burton L.
    Business report writing.

    Includes index.
    1.   Business report writing.   I.   Title.
HF5719.F57   1975   808'.066'651748   75-20317
ISBN 0-913310-40-9

CONTENTS

CHAPTER 1
COMMUNICATIONS TODAY

The Exciting World of Business

Today, more than ever before, the world of business has become a stimulating and dynamic place in which to work. For many people, their appreciation of business is limited to that which they learn in their role as consumers. As a consumer, one views the world of business from the perspective of a shopper or user only. But—actually *being in the center* of business—the center from which action starts and decisions are made—is exciting, challenging, and demanding.

What is Business?

What is business? What does the term *business* mean? Any situation in which human beings are involved in the exchange of goods and services can be construed to be "business." Business means any occupation for which profit is the goal and in which there is a risk of loss.

From this general definition, we can understand that business can be a much more all-inclusive thing than we sometimes realize.

To get more specific, the pursuit of business may signify many functions: buying and selling, production and distribution, trading and transacting, marketing, wholesaling and retailing. These different functions of business begin to give us a feeling of the length and breadth of business.

The Formal Business Organization

Thus far, we have been talking about a general definition and the different functions of business.

Business does not exist in a vacuum. Business ordinarily resides in an organization whose activities include providing *goods and services*. We know, too, that some business firms are large and extensive, and that some are small and limited.

Free Enterprise Systems

In the Free World, government regulations and limitations regarding business are general in nature and ordinarily not restrictive. And—there is plenty of opportunity for new businesses of all sorts to compete with one another.

In the United States, the number of different kinds of businesses has grown to such an extent that it is virtually impossible to keep track of each and every type of business.

In Communist countries, the government limits the number and kinds of businesses. Strictly speaking, there is no "business" as we know it—in a competitive sense. The government plans, produces, distributes, and provides for the goods and services of the people.

In the United States and those countries which encourage or allow for the free enterprise system, anyone can go into business for himself—provided he has the necessary means in money and ideas to make a success of his venture. And—immediate capital is not necessarily a limitation. Credit systems allow for a great deal of creativity and ingenuity in business.

Basic Business Structure

Every business, regardless of its size, has a basic structure. This structure consists of the following: First, the *investor* or *owner* who supplies the money or purchases the stocks in the company.

Next, there are the *upper-level managers* or *executives* who manage the company or firm.

Then, there are those who produce the goods or provide the services, the *workmen.*

And, finally, there is the public—the *consumers*—who purchase and use the goods and services.

By now, technology has generated a great deal of progress in all lines of endeavor. It is both exciting and informative to consider the various kinds of new businesses that have come into being in the last decade.

Now do Assignments #1 and #2 on pages 12 — 13

The Administration and Organization of Business

Businesses move in many different ways. However, regardless of any superficial variation in business structures, there are basic ways in which most businesses operate.

If you were setting up a business, there are certain things you would have to do in order to make a success of your business.

The first thing you would have to do would be to set up a goal or *objective* which you and your company would pursue. Money or profit would certainly be part of it. But—within a general area—you would have to decide upon a particular kind of goods or service that you would like to provide. And, of course, you would be keenly interested in operating your company in such a way as to make a success—and a profit.

You did some of this kind of thinking and planning in Assignment #2 in this chapter.

Further—in order to successfully achieve your *objective*, there are certain things that you would have to do. First, you would have to do some sort of *planning*. A certain amount of *planning* is necessary so that your company would have a road-map to follow.

2

Second, there must be some division of work responsibility. The people who are working for you cannot all do the same thing; nor can you leave it for them to decide who will do what. You would have to set up an *organization*—an *organization* of work responsibilities.

Third, to get your business functioning (that is to say, the *organization* of people following through with your plan) there would have to be an *administration*—the sector of your business organization which would manage and move your company towards its goal.

Finally, in order to discover whether or not the organization is pursuing the company plans effectively, there must be *control and evaluation*.

One of the important means of accomplishing *control and evaluation* is the subject of this book: Report Writing.

In order to check the manner in which the organization is proceeding towards the company goal, in relationship to that which is projected, there must be communication of results on just what is happening. Therefore, report writing and the general topic of communication are very much related to a basic part of the administration and organization of business which is, again, *control and evaluation*.

The Importance of Communication

To gauge or measure its progress, a company or corporation needs ways of looking objectively at its progress in relationship to its goal. And it is the responsibility of managers to communicate—to keep in touch with each other—via different communication media.

In order for each of the various divisions in an organization to know what the other is doing, the working relationship of men, money and materials must be talked about and written about.

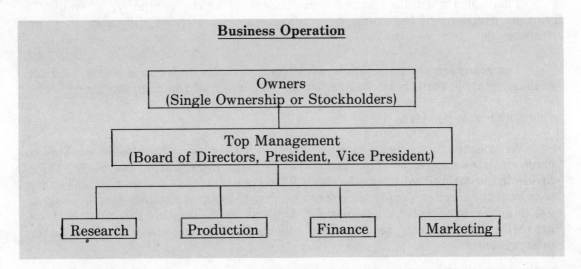

The diagram above is an overview of a typical large-scale business and how it operates.

A company may be owned by a *single owner* or it may be owned by hundreds or thousands of *stockholders*.

Top management has to make the basic policy decisions which the company pursues for the benefit of the ownership.

The *president*, along with the *vice presidents*, has the responsibility of pursuing company objectives. The vice presidents must answer to the president.

The *research division* has the responsibility of designing and improving products, as well as the responsibility of seeking better and more efficient ways of dealing with the materials that are to be used for production.

Production is responsible for the making of the products. It must locate the plants or factories, equip the plants, set up production schedules, purchase materials, hire and train the labor to do the job, as well as the many other things that must go into *production*.

Those in the *finance division* take care of the financial or money responsibilities—handling problems that are connected with credit, billing, collection of money, paying bills, paying salaries, keeping records and tending to state and federal government tax obligations.

And, finally, the *marketing division* deals with setting prices for the products or service, and handles advertising, sales, and research into the saleability and useability of the products and services in which the company deals.

Regardless of whether the company is large or small, regular communication between and among the various divisions of the company is a necessity.

This process is known as *horizontal communication* when the different divisions of a company or corporation communicate with each other.

There also must be *vertical communication* in the company, whereby the various divisions of the company communicate with those to whom they are responsible.

Top management must know what each division under it is doing, and top management, in turn, must answer to the ownership of the company.

Competition in Business

What keeps business on its toes? What is it that keeps businesses working to communicate effectively? What keeps the company organization pulsating? What drives it to continue working effectively? Two possible answers are that either the people in the company enjoy their work or that they must do their jobs in order to get paid. From a better point of view, the answer is that complacency in business—that is, remaining *too* calm and collected—is dangerous in the Free Enterprise system.

The nature of competition in business in the United States and in the free world is such that a company, whether it is large or small, which takes its success for granted may find itself forced out of business or into a weak financial condition by failing to deliver its goods or services at the same level as competing companies. And, since competition is a constant factor to consider—particularly with improvement in technology and in the operation of businesses—those companies which do not keep pace with a changing world will find themselves in difficulty.

Competition in American businesses acts as a greater control than the government, in many respects. Businessmen, knowing that they have competition, strive to provide quality products and service in order to keep up with their competitors. In the United States, most businesses have competition.

Even the telephone company, long a legal monopoly, no longer enjoys an exclusive right. It, too, finds that it must compete in quality and service with new innovational techniques, procedures and facilities provided by competitive telephone companies.

Communication

"Communication," in recent years, has become a much used term in the English language. For example, "Communication gap" is something that has been referred to a great deal in the area of relations between the generations.

Problems regarding communication in general have been talked about extensively in education, industry, and government.

What *is* communication? Communication is the process of *sending* and *receiving* information. As you will notice in the diagram below, in the communication process there is a *sender*, a *message*, a *medium*, and a *receiver*.

Communication Process

Sender		Message		Medium		Receiver
(The person or company sending the message.)	→	("What" the person or company wants to say.)	→	(The means or channel selected to convey the message, such as: report, letter, memo, etc.)	→	(The individual, people, or company for whom the message is intended.)

The Communication Process

All parts of the communication process are important. Communication is a process that is complete *only when:*

1) there is a responsible *sender* who knows what he or she wants to say;

2) he or she has a clear *message* intended;

3) there is an effective choice of *media* or the "right" communication channel; and

4) the *receiver*, the individual, the group, the people, or the company get the message as intended by the sender.

Regular, effective communication is very important. Successful projection of our ideas, pictures, thoughts, or feelings is a constant challenge to us all.

As communication has been studied more and more thoroughly in recent years, we have discovered that new inventions spurred on by technology do not necessarily make the communication process any easier. The challenge for clarity to the *sender* and the *receiver* has increased with the social changes taking place around us.

Aside from the actual use of technological media like the telephone, radio, telegraph, TV, we, as people, communicate in different ways.

There is oral communication (speaking), written communication (writing), and non-verbal communication (sometimes called "body language").

No one means of communication is more important than another. The individual who wishes to excel as a communicator must constantly be on guard to see that his or her own approach to communication is the best for the situation with which he or she is faced. The process of communication should be completed to the satisfaction of both the receiver *and* the sender.

Oral Communication

A great part of our active communication is in the oral or speaking medium. In a typical day most of us do the large part of our communication with the spoken word. And we usually *hear* more words than we read.

In the contemporary business world, good speech is of great importance. The spoken word is constantly at work. The intercom system, the telephone (with all its new variations), and—most important—personal contact, all demand good speech.

Businessmen today are constantly in and out of meetings. Meetings may be by telephone or in person. There are interviews, conferences, and large-scale meetings. Meetings of all sizes demand that people going into business be able to communicate effectively through the spoken word.

The Strengths and Weaknesses of Oral Communication

There are many challenges to effective oral communication. Both the speaker (sender) and the listener (receiver) are challenged if they wish to participate profitably in the process of communication.

Now do Assignment #3 on page 14

6

As we observed above, oral communication is used extensively throughout organized business. It does not take much argument to prove that being a good speaker is an asset to anyone who wants to succeed in society today.

We should be aware also of the limitations of oral communication—particularly when we need a permanent record of information or data. For record keeping, precision, and sometimes convenience we need to think of *written communication.*

Written communication also has the advantage of allowing the individual to read and think about the message quietly and privately, as well as in a group. A great quantity of our communication in everyday life is in writing or printing.

Most of us have had experience in writing from the earliest years on up through high school. However, as with oral communication, there is not a good writer who cannot become a better one. And because of the challenge of change and the complexities of industry today, we need to work at improving our ability to write. We cannot take for granted our skills in this communication area.

Few of us are satisfied with our capacity as writers. Finding that elusive "right" word and expressing it in the "right" way is a daily challenge to every present and future businessman.

You the Supervisor

With your college training, you will either become a supervisor or work closely with one. The tremendous amount of paperwork in industry today makes it necessary for the effective worker to be able to deal responsibly and accurately with written communication.

The supervisor or his assistant must be able to make his writing clear and coherent, and write according to acceptable standards. He must be able to write so that people will be able to read his work and analyze his information intelligently.

The kinds of reports that a supervisor is called upon to write may vary from very short to very lengthy ones. They may range from simple reports on production and evaluations of personnel performance on a daily or weekly basis to the quarterly and annual reports on progress in production, marketing, and accounting.

Typically, workers are not hired for their writing ability. Ordinarily, they are hired for abilities to perform a particular function in a company. The ability to write a report when called upon is simply assumed by the owner, supervisor, or personnel office which hires you.

Regardless of how you get your position, once in there, rest assured that you will be called upon to write one kind of report or another.

Now do Assignment #4 on page 15

Telecommunications

What does the term *telecommunications* mean? What relevance do the new breakthroughs in telecommunications have for the businessman and business communication?

Telecommunications has to do with those communication media which project messages from a distance. The field includes: the telephone, the telegraph and television. The field ranges in difficulty from the simplest intercom system to the most complex satellite communications arrangement.

Many new telecommunications devices have come into being in recent years. Some of the newer items in the field include: videotelephones, interactive television, electronic mail, and new data systems. These things are coming into being and in some cases are in use. They are the results of new scientific research and development. There is tremendous use for them in business as they become available.

Of all the electronic hardware being developed, the variations on the telephone are probably the most practical and will probably get the most use. There are several reasons for this. First, the telephone is universally available, and is by far the least expensive electronic communication terminal. Second, people have learned to use the telephone expertly instead of, or as an alternative to, personal contact. Third, the telephone effectively meets many of today's and tomorrow's communication needs.

So it is the telephone—of those communication media which project messages from afar—which many find most interesting and practical to talk about.

The following commentary will explain some of the variations on the telephone which will be of interest to the business student.

The Videotelephone

The videotelephone is a promising possibility. For high-level discussion in which both parties are prepared to devote their full attention, the videotelephone is a meaningful device. With business organizations, its use will probably be confined to top executives.

The videotelephone will be particularly appropriate for external communication by top management—for example, calls to presidents or vice-presidents of one company to those of another, major customers, legislators, and key employees overseas. In such cases, the caller wants to leave no doubt that he is giving his full attention to the call and that he also has an important purpose for placing the call.

For the average business or organization, the videotelephone will be too expensive an item because a toll call on a videotelephone uses facilities that might otherwise carry ninety-six voice calls. For another thing, facial features and expressions add little to the information exchange between two people who are well known to each other. Finally, when a person is "on camera," he cannot simultaneously perform other activities, such as signing letters or reading correspondence.

Overall, the videotelephone has powerful but limited potential for business.

Interconnect

A radical departure from what we have come to know as the traditional use of the telephone lies in the *interconnect industry*.

Until 1968, little was known about the "Interconnect" industry. At that time, the F.C.C. (Federal Communications Commission) in its historic "Carterfone" decision, ruled that Bell Telephone must allow any telecommunications equipment to be connected to its lines. This decision led the way for many innovations in the communication field, and made it possible for the consumer actually to own telecommunications equipment. This decision opened the way for newer and more sophisticated systems which can do a communication job efficiently and less expensively.

The Carterfone decision can perhaps be best explained by comparing telephone equipment to any home appliance. In the same way that one purchases appliances and operates them using a public utility, one can now purchase telephone equipment and use Bell Telephone lines as one would use electricity or gas. Evidence of the desirability of "interconnect" can be found in its burgeoning growth. From the birth of "interconnect" in 1968, sales grew to 40 million dollars in 1970. Projected sales for 1980 are 1.3 billion dollars.

These dramatic figures represent not only the desire on the part of the business world to take advantage of "interconnect," but also the demand for privately owned telephone companies such as Tele-Comm and the National Telephone Company.

Here are two of the features of these new interconnect telephones—features not available ordinarily for regular telephone equipment: Add-on conference and optional music.

Add-On Conference

On incoming extended calls, the call station having once placed the outside party on "hold" may consult privately with another internal station and then add-on the outside party for up to a three-party conference.

Optional Music on Hold

The music feature provides that a predetermined melody be sent to the holding party as long as the call remains on "hold."

Technology has also developed mobile telephones for automobiles, portable telephones which can be carried in brief cases or attaché cases, and "thought tanks." "Thought tanks" are central recording stations or equipment for dictation—into which supervisors can call in—by telephone—memos, letters, and reports.

Some of these breakthroughs in technology are interesting, and in some cases quite practical. They can mean savings in cost and improved communications for many businesses and organizations.

The telecommunications industry is very exciting. One can learn a great deal by studying what is happening in it.

Summary

In this chapter we have talked about the exciting world of business, the nature of business, the nature of the Free Enterprise System, basic business structure, and functions performed by divisions in business organizations. We talked about the strengths and weaknesses of oral communication and the necessity of effective written communication. We also talked about telecommunications and the many new technological media which have burgeoned out of the scientific age in which we live.

In the next chapter we will be addressing ourselves to the more specific communication responsibilities that confront us in business organizations; particularly: Reporting to Your Supervisor.

Questions for Research and Discussion

Communication is an extensive field of study. There are, of course, many challenging fields of study—psychology, philosophy, political science, and others. Communication differs from other fields in its focus on the *process* of exchanging information. Studies in communication concentrate on the how, what, and why of the *communication process*.

With your teacher serving as a resource guide, study, research, and express your opinions on the topics designated below.

You may want to write reports on one or more of these topics; or you may simply plan to discuss your findings and opinions in class.

1. **Barriers to Communication** — What is "open" communication? What are some barriers to good communication? How can we overcome some of the barriers that get in the way of good "open" communication?

2. **Dependence on Technology** — Suppose we had an energy crisis that wiped out electricity in the United States. And suppose this crisis eliminated the use of the telephone and other electronic communication media. Could we

survive? What would we do? How well do you think we would do? What are some of the problems we might encounter?

3. **Non-Verbal Language** — Suppose we could no longer communicate with words. Could we communicate with non-verbal or "body language"? Could we make it on "body language" alone? Make a list of body movements or facial expressions and note what they communicate.

4. **The Government and Communication** — To what extent does the government control what we hear and what we read? Do we really have free communication in our society? Is there censorship in our country? To what extent is there censorship of the communication media?

5. **Change and the English Language** — In what ways have you noticed that the language we speak has changed? Have people been using slang *more* to communicate in recent years? Is this good or bad? Why?

6. **Radio** — In what ways has radio changed as a means of communication? Is radio the same now as the way you remember it when you were younger? Why? How? In what way? Aside from pictures, how does radio differ from television?

7. **Television** — Television is a very powerful part of the communication media today. How does television affect you? Does television control people's minds? If you could change television, how would you change it? In what ways? If you owned a TV station, how would your television station differ from others?

8. **Telephone** — How much do people use the telephone? Why? Has the telephone opened up communication for you? Socially? Professionally? Educationally? Explain your opinion.

9. **Oral Communication in Meetings** — How do you think business meetings should be conducted? In what ways would you improve business meetings? Assume you were just hired by a company as a supervisor, and you were asked to plan the next meeting, what steps would you go through to ensure that the next meeting would be a success?

10. **Business** — How do people with large businesses use the different communication media? How and in what ways would a small business owner use communication media? Which ones would he be likely to use? Why? If you were the owner of a big business, what *new* ways would you use communication media to help run your business?

ASSIGNMENT #1

Instructions: For your next class, look through newspapers, magazines, and the classified telephone directory for the names of five businesses which strike you as interesting.

In **Column A** write the name and address of each company.

In **Column B** write a brief description of the goods or services each company provides.

Be ready to discuss your research for your next class.

Column A	**Column B**
Name of New Business	Goods or Services Provided by the Company

1._____   _____

  _____   _____

  _____   _____

2._____   _____

  _____   _____

  _____   _____

3._____   _____

  _____   _____

  _____   _____

4._____   _____

  _____   _____

  _____   _____

5._____   _____

  _____   _____

  _____   _____

ASSIGNMENT #2

Instructions: To be a success in business, one must have a certain amount of imagination and daring. Assume you have won a large sum of money in a lottery. Wanting to put your money to good use, you want to start your own business.

On the blanks below write the name of an original company (your company), a geographical location, and some ideas on the kinds of goods or services your company could provide.

_____

Name of Your Company:_____

Location of Your Company:_____

_____

Goods or Services your company will provide:_____

_____

_____

_____

_____

_____

_____

_____

_____

_____

_____

_____

_____

_____

_____

ASSIGNMENT #3

Instructions: Each medium of communication has its problems. And there are problem areas or "barriers" to effective communication.

In **Column A**, write what you consider to be a barrier to good oral communication. In **Column B**, write a brief description of that barrier. Once you have listed and discussed some of the problems of oral communication, you will become more clearly aware of the advantages and disadvantages of the medium of oral communication.

Column A   Column B

1. _____

2. _____

3. _____

4. _____

5. _____

ASSIGNMENT #4

Instructions: On the lines below, list in **Column A** what you consider to be a barrier to good *written communication.* In **Column B**, write a brief description of that barrier. *For example:* **Column A—** Vocabulary; **Column B**—some people use words others don't understand, and this cuts down on good communications.

Once you have listed and discussed some of the problems of written communication, you will become more clearly aware of the advantages and disadvantages of written communication.

Column A   **Column B**

1. _____   _____

   _____   _____

   _____

   _____

2. _____   _____

   _____   _____

   _____

   _____

3. _____   _____

   _____   _____

   _____

   _____

4. _____   _____

   _____   _____

   _____

   _____

5. _____   _____

   _____   _____

   _____

   _____

CHAPTER 2

REPORTING TO YOUR SUPERVISOR

The Job of the Supervisor

Various styles of living and working have been attempted in the contemporary age. In some cases, the results of these new styles have been favorable. The people involved have found greater profit and personal satisfaction in the way they now work.

However, both in the conservative, as well as some of the liberal or radical attempts at life style and work style, it has been discovered by both young and old that there is need for *organization*. There must be a structure within which the people involved live and work.

Reports on communes have stressed the fact that only those communes which have had an objective clearly in mind have survived. Only those communes which have done some deliberate planning for their work and well-being have "made it." Only those communes which are organized and have some sort of systematic administration thrive. Only those communes which control and evaluate their progress have succeeded in their aspirations to live independently. Others, mostly, have fallen by the wayside, have disintegrated, or have openly disbanded.

The reader will recall that in Chapter 1 we pointed out that administration and organization are basic to any business. And this is valid regardless of whether the profits are shared in common—as in a commune—or given to the ownership—as in the typical business operation.

In the successful commune, as in any effective organization, there are other parallels as well. There is, for instance, a need for supervision. There must be someone to oversee things—someone to take the responsibility for production. There must be a *supervisor*.

However good the intentions of the workers, someone must serve as guide to the operation. In the organization of people in the real world, the supervisor is a necessity.

What is a Supervisor?

In general, a supervisor is one who oversees the work of others. The supervisor is an individual who works for the benefit of the ownership. He is immediately above his subordinates in the organizational hierarchy. Frequently, the term *supervisor* refers to a first-line manager who directs the activities of operative-level employees. Most, if not all, workers have to report to somebody.

In the work-a-day business world few of us do not have to report to a department head, a director, a superintendent, or an executive.

Reporting

How does one report to a supervisor? There are different basic ways in which we can report to a supervisor. We may file, send, mail, or in general provide a report for our supervisors. In this chapter we will consider four basic means which we are likely to use in giving a report: 1) telephone, 2) interview, 3) memorandum, and 4) written report.

As the reader will observe, these four means of communication divide into two categories—the two main categories of communication we talked about in Chapter 1: *Oral Communication* and *Written Communication.*

First, let us consider telephoning the supervisor.

Telephoning the Supervisor

Why telephone your supervisor? First, it is not always efficient in terms of the effective use of time to report to a supervisor in person. The nature of the business in which you work may be such that you will have to be in another geographical location—working away from the immediate vicinity of the office out of which you work. Or, it is quite possible that the situation could be reversed. The supervisor could be out of the immediate vicinity of the home office, and you may have to rely on the telephone in order to speak with him. In either case, because of your respective locations, it may be best to use the telephone as your channel of communication.

Another reason for the use of the telephone is that written communication is not always the fastest means of communication. This is true for a number of reasons. First, written communication—whether in the form of a memorandum or of a formal written report—takes a good deal of time to prepare. There may be two or more people involved in the preparation of a written report. You, the originator of the report, and a secretary or others may be needed to do the actual typing of the report.

Another advantage of oral communication is speed. There can be a faster interaction between the two parties communicating than would ordinarily be possible in written communication.

In the oral report, then, you are providing information, suggestions, or recommendations about a particular problem or area of work. You are doing so by speech and by means of the telephone.

The Telephone

The telephone has the advantage of being a quick and easy-to-use medium for brief, oral communication. However, there are some guidelines which the student should keep in mind in planning to use the telephone. First, it is a good idea to prepare oneself with a pencil or pen, and a pad or record book, so that words, ideas, information, or data which are exchanged on the telephone can be noted while the communication is going on. And, too, the efficient businessperson should note the particular *date* on which the communication was taking place.

Then there is the cost factor. While most, if not all, businesses appreciate that good communication is important, inevitably the question of the cost involved will be raised. Although the supervisor wants to have good, efficient communication by way of the telephone, he is also likely to want to keep the cost of such communication to a minimum.

The telephone company allows for various kinds of services for local and long-distance calls. Listed below are the various types of calls that can be made. The effective businessperson should familiarize himself with the advantages of these different kinds of calls and select the service which would allow him to communicate effectively as well as economically.

1. Station-to-Station
2. Person-to-Person
3. Nights and Sundays
4. Messenger Calls
5. Conference Calls
6. Mobile Telephone Service
7. Overseas and Ship-to-Shore Calls
8. Private-Line Telephone Services
9. WATS (Wide Area Telephone Service)

Convenience Aids for Telephone Use

There are many convenience aids and equipment which the telephone company makes available. An investigation of the resources at your disposal will prove to be practical.

Now do Assignment #5 on page 25

Reporting by Interview

An interview is a face-to-face form of communication between a worker and a supervisor. An interview is a conversation or verbal exchange usually between two people for a particular purpose.

The interview allows for conversation and question for the purpose of generating information. The interview may be held for the purpose of giving one's opinion, holding an inquiry, giving an oral examination, or getting something "straight for the record."

The interview is a very good way in which to report to a supervisor, for it provides an opportunity to tell and show with the spoken word, gestures, and facial expressions. The in-person exchange of two—a supervisor and a subordinate—can be a challenge to the speed of thinking. It has the advantage of allowing you and your supervisor to learn more about each other as well as to transact information on a particular point. From the foregoing paragraphs you can see that the interview has many advantages.

For a change of pace, for the purpose of keeping communication in a company going at a high level, and for building morale, the interview is often desirable.

The interview also has a disadvantage: it will ordinarily require a bigger time block than you may want to allow for in a given business day.

There are two sides to the successful interview. One is speaking, and the other is listening. In order to have an effective interview, some consideration should be given to both the art of listening and the art of speaking.

Interview Preparation

It is easy to underestimate the necessity of coming prepared to an interview. It may not be necessary to prepare to the extent that one would in getting ready to address a group with a formal speech, but this does not mean that one should not come properly prepared to an interview.

If the businessperson wants to progress in a company, make a good impression, and communicate effectively, he very definitely needs to prepare for the interview.

There are certain basic areas which contribute to the success of an interview (or conference) with a supervisor. The following topics and the explanations which accompany them will help the student do a better job of speaking and listening in the interview.

Speaking

1. Outline

    Prepare an outline of the report you are going to give in your interview or conference with your supervisor. An outline is simply a map designating where you are going. In the case of the interview, it will guide you in what you are going to communicate. There are many ways to outline. Use the pattern which is most comfortable for you. A sentence or phrase outline of your topics and subtopics will probably do the job for you.

2. Time Limits

    Find out how much time you are being given for the interview. Then get your general subject in mind. Do not memorize what you are going to say; rather, your purpose is to become confident and prepared for what it is you are going to say in a general, rather than in an overly specific way.

3. Organization

Put your ideas in an order which will dress up what you are going to say to the best advantage. Then, keep it simple; sometimes a business report will focus on one point. However, it is perfectly all right to make several points. But caution—do not overcomplicate an issue and confuse your supervisor regarding what you want to say. Three points ordinarily is a good number to shoot for.

4. Clarify Your Message

Be sure to provide enough points or details so that your supervisor will understand what you want to say. And use graphs, charts, or visual aids to help him visualize what you are talking about.

5. Be Persuasive

It is an advantage to speak well. It is also an advantage to be articulate, clear, and easy to understand. However, be sure to be enthusiastic and persuasive in presenting your message. Enthusiasm incorporated into your voice will ordinarily help you get your message across.

6. Conclude Well

Make it clear to your listener that you have made your point and you are ready to hear his response. Do not leave him hanging in the air. Let him know by voice or manner that you have presented the message with which you came to the interview.

Listening

Just as important as speaking is to the effective interview is skill in listening. Remember that looking as if one were listening is not listening. Be sensitive to the response of your supervisor to whatever you have to say to him. And concentrate on what he says in return.

1. Body Language

All kinds of signs from your supervisor can be a guide to the effectiveness of your communication with him. A raise of the eyebrows may signify something. Frowns, laughter, yawns, glances at the clock, and many other bits of behavior can guide you as to whether or not you should speak faster, slower, softer, louder, or make qualifications on the subject about which you are reporting.

2. Specific Questions

The best advice on specific questions is to listen carefully to them. If you are asked a specific question by a supervisor, be sure to listen to it. Often it is a good idea to ask to have the question repeated, rather than ramble on foolishly and not answer the question. The supervisor will not be offended by being asked to repeat a question. He will appreciate your intent to respond directly to his query.

3. Nondirective Question

The nondirective question is distinct from the specific question in that it is asked in part to help the speaker "open up." It is sometimes more difficult to respond to in that the nondirective question leaves it to the speaker to organize his own thoughts. The general nondirective question leaves it to the speaker to be specific on his own.

Now do Assignment #6 on page 27

Writing a Memorandum

A memorandum is a form of communication in which something that needs to be remembered is written down. Ordinarily, a memorandum is characterized by informality, and it is used as a reminder in business of a particular information, an act, or an event. The memorandum is not considered a forceful means of communication and is not customarily used as a basis for action; rather, it is often used as a record of action.

A memorandum can also be used as a means of distributing notes regarding reminders of appointments and responsibilities. Typically a memorandum is an inter-office or intra-company written form of communication.

The memorandum is similar to a letter or an informal report in that it usually follows a predetermined form at the introductory section.

The introductory section shows who originated the memorandum, to whom it is addressed, the subject matter, and the date. The specimen which follows is an example of a typical memorandum—illustrative both in form and content of a common business situation.

MEMO

TO: Mr. Robert L. Montgomery
Plant Superintendent

DATE: December 4, 19--

FROM: C. L. Pierce

SUBJECT: New Coffee Break

A conference with the line foreman today produced a new time arrangement for the morning coffee break.

This coming Monday, December 7, the line personnel will begin taking their fifteen-minute coffee breaks starting at 9:45 a.m.

This new arrangement will allow the last group to finish its break in time for the kitchen staff to set up for lunch.

This should alleviate the complaints we have had from the production and kitchen personnel.

C.L.P.

THE MEMORANDUM ABOVE WILL GIVE THE STUDENT A FEELING FOR BOTH THE FORM AND CONTENT OF BUSINESS MEMOS. NOTICE THE PLACEMENT OF "DATE," "TO," "FROM," AND "SUBJECT." OBSERVE THE BREVITY OF THE MESSAGE WHICH ESSENTIALLY RECORDS THE RESULTS OF A CONFERENCE AND THE ACTION TO BE TAKEN.

Now do Assignment #7 on page 29

Writing Reports

Report writing is the subject of this entire book. It is a most challenging topic for beginners, as well as experienced people in business.

In reports information, suggestions, and recommendations of interest to the company are prepared in written form and submitted to a supervisor.

Written reports are regularly written throughout the world on technical as well as simple matters in business. The well-organized business report can be the most thorough and complete way of communicating in industry.

Since report writing is the subject of this text, it will be dealt with in detail in the forthcoming chapters. However, in this chapter we will make a beginning to help the student become familiar with the basic problems of communicating with the supervisor by written report.

What is a Report?

A report is an account or statement describing in detail an event or situation. Usually, a report is the result of observation and inquiry—for example, a report on a fire or a medical report on a heart patient.

It is probably obvious to you that such reports will be more detailed than the simple inter-office memo. The difference between a short report and a memorandum can be minimal at times. More often, however, there will be a conspicuous difference.

Some of the ways in which a formal report will differ from a memo is that a report will include recommendations, data, plan of action, and some accompanying discussion.

The concluding assignment in this chapter is provided as an opportunity for the student to "jump" into the problems of report writing.

Now do Assignment #8 on page 30

ASSIGNMENT #5

Instructions: In order to get a more specific appreciation of the services, materials, information, personnel, and equipment available to you, consult the white pages of your telephone directory under "General Information" for this assignment.

For your next class, look under the headings indicated below and fill in some information after each topic based on your research of the telephone directory. If you have any difficulty finding this information, ask to speak to a communications consultant at the telephone company. Or ask your instructor for assistance.

1. Communication Consultant: _____

_____

_____

_____

2. Tours and Visitors: _____

_____

_____

_____

3. When you hear beep tone: _____

_____

_____

_____

4. Customer-provided equipment: _____

_____

_____

_____

5. Employee Identification Card: _____

_____

_____

_____

6. Telegrams by Telephone: _____

_____

_____

_____

7. Directories: _____

_____

_____

_____

8. Personal Directory: _____

_____

_____

_____

9. Out-of-Town Directories: _____

_____

_____

_____

10. Usage of Service: _____

_____

_____

_____

ASSIGNMENT #6

Instructions: Prepare for and go to an interview with a supervisor who works in a business organization in which you are interested.

Prepare yourself by using this worksheet. Design specific questions with which you expect to approach the interview.

Go to the placement bureau, the career planning office at your school, or the library and find out everything you can about a company in your area. Then by using these sources or by calling the company, find out about the role of a particular supervisor at this company. Then design the questions with which you plan to interview the supervisor on the lines below.

You may want to prepare a written report on your interview, or you may simply want to report orally on your interview to your class.

_____

1. Question: _____

    _____

    _____

    _____

    Response: _____

    _____

    _____

    _____

2. Question: _____

    _____

    _____

    _____

    Response: _____

    _____

    _____

    _____

3. Question: _____

_____

_____

_____

Response: _____

_____

_____

_____

4. Question: _____

_____

_____

_____

Response: _____

_____

_____

_____

5. Question: _____

_____

_____

_____

Response: _____

_____

_____

_____

ASSIGNMENT #7

Instructions: Assume that you have been asked by your supervisor to do something about a problem in your section. *For example:* that there has been an over-use **of the Xerox machine, that there** has been excessive use of secretarial supplies, that there has been too much absenteeism, or that there have been too many people coming in late for work.

Your supervisor has asked you to do something about the problem. You have had a conference with the personnel involved and now you want to communicate to him the results of the conference and the action to be taken.

MEMO

TO: **DATE:**

FROM:

SUBJECT:

_____

_____

_____

_____

_____

_____

_____

_____

_____

_____

_____

_____

_____

_____

ASSIGNMENT #8

Instructions: Assume that your supervisor has asked you to come up with a recommendation for one of the following situations:

1.   Your group wants to have a luncheon at a restaurant and an investigation needs to be done on this topic.

2.   Six electric typewriters are needed in the office and you are asked to investigate and recommend the best model for your company. Either assume you are working for a particular company or do your research for a company with which you are familiar.

3.   New dictation cassettes are needed in your office and you are asked to investigate the possibilities and make a recommendation.

4.   A new photocopy service is needed and you are asked to check out the alternatives and make a recommendation.

Go to the actual companies and take notes appropriate to the nature of your report. Later, refine your notes, organize your thinking, and fill in the details called for on the report form which follows.

There is an additional report form included should you wish to do an additional report.

REPORT

TO: DATE:

FROM:

SUBJECT:

RECOMMENDATIONS: _____

_____

_____

_____

_____

DATA: _____

_____

_____

_____

_____

PLAN OF ACTION: _____

_____

_____

_____

DISCUSSION: _____

_____

_____

_____

_____

_____

_____

_____

_____

_____

_____

_____

_____

_____

_____

_____

_____

_____

REPORT

TO: DATE:

FROM:

SUBJECT:

_____

RECOMMENDATIONS: _____

_____

_____

_____

_____

DATA: _____

_____

_____

_____

PLAN OF ACTION: _____

_____

_____

_____

DISCUSSION: _____

_____

_____

_____

_____

_____

_____

_____

REPORT

TO: _____ DATE: _____

FROM: _____

SUBJECT: _____

_____

RECOMMENDATIONS: _____

_____

_____

_____

_____

DATA: _____

_____

_____

_____

PLAN OF ACTION: _____

_____

_____

_____

DISCUSSION: _____

_____

_____

_____

_____

_____

_____

_____

REPORT

TO: _____   DATE: _____

FROM: _____

SUBJECT: _____

_____

RECOMMENDATIONS: _____

_____

_____

_____

_____

DATA: _____

_____

_____

_____

PLAN OF ACTION: _____

_____

_____

_____

DISCUSSION: _____

_____

_____

_____

_____

_____

_____

_____

_____

34

CHAPTER 3
THE PURPOSE OF A REPORT

Producing a good report, whether it is a brief, informal one, or a lengthy, detailed formal report, is a definite challenge to the business student and the businessman.

There are many reasons for studying report writing. In this chapter we will consider the general as well as specific reasons for studying report writing.

The Value of Studying Report Writing

One general reason for studying report writing is that it is a challenge for the mind. One must think through a given situation. Report writing forces the individual to "put up or shut up." That is to say, writing a report forces the individual to be concrete and specific about ideas, recommendations, information, and ability.

At the outset, the student should realize that writing is a challenge. Some help in the matter is appreciated by the best of writers. There isn't a good writer who can't become a better one.

The kinds of problems one encounters in writing reports have a value or transfer of value in other areas in which one is called upon to write. The challenge of communicating through the medium of a report is characteristic not only of business but of academic programs on all levels—beginning, advanced and graduate.

One value of studying report writing, in general, is that it will aid and facilitate *your* progress as a student in college now, in advanced college training, and in training programs which you may enter outside of college.

Thus, learning to communicate effectively by means of a report can be a helpful experience in intellectual growth as well as in your ability to successfully complete training programs of all sorts.

Getting a Job

Writing a resumé or report on your background in order to get a job will call upon your writing skills—skills that you are also called upon to use in effective report writing.

Furthermore, it is not unusual to be asked directly by a personnel interviewer or employer whether or not you can, indeed, write a report. In some instances, candidates for jobs are asked for samples of reports they have written, though it should be pointed out that this is unusual.

Some college placement personnel report that recruiters coming on campus have been known to ask whether or not the individual can write reports and whether or not he has had a course in report writing.

The emphasis that employers place on report writing before one gets the job underscores the value business places on report writing.

Report Writing on the Job

Once on the job, an employee is called upon to write reports for a variety of reasons. There are specific purposes, goals, and objectives which management has in mind when it calls upon you to write a report.

We will consider four basic purposes for which you may be called upon to write a report, and give you some experience in the practice of writing reports.

Communicating Ideas

A real part of the business environment is a request from your supervisor to provide him with impressions, opinions, or ideas which are not necessarily bound in by definitive recommendations or extensive research.

A report which is idea-centered may be preliminary in nature. You may be a scientist, an engineer, or a technician. Your supervisor may be planning to give you a new project or problem, and he may simply be interested in knowing your intentions. That is to say, he may be interested in knowing how you propose to go about a particular project or work assignment.

Subsequent to receiving a preliminary report there may be a conference or interview at which you will have to report more thoroughly and in detail.

But for the moment, all he may want in a written report may be some preliminary ideas on how you plan to handle the project.

You may be one or one of a number who are being invited to put down in writing suggestions for production, sales, or research for the benefit of the company. Because this kind of report is not necessarily lengthy does not mean that it may not be an important part of your work with the company.

The "right" idea effectively and persuasively presented in a report can do much to enhance your position in the company. An effective report of this order may bring you into prominence in the company. It can also be personally gratifying to have recommended a good idea. And, last but not least, sometimes the presentation of good ideas or good suggestions can earn an individual a cash reward or an improvement in salary range.

Now do Assignment #9 on page 41

Communicating Recommendations

A report which includes recommendations is an aggressive kind of report. You are involved in decision-making at a certain level, depending on your status in the organization. Here your supervisor is looking for more than suggestions and ideas. He is expecting you to specify the course of action which seems to be called for in the situation. Your supervisor will be looking for you to advocate a particular move. He may be looking for general or specific direction from you. He may be looking for a proposal, a judgment, an endorsement, or support for a particular move that the company or the department is getting ready to make.

It could very well be an "off" or "on" situation — a "yes" or "no" situation — depending on what is involved. The situation may involve buying some new equipment and new machines, adding on personnel, adding a new product to the line, moving the entire office or company to a new location. Requests for new equipment or personnel and the accompanying recommendations regarding them are a very common occurrence in business.

The way or ways in which you justify your recommendation may very well be questioned. Consequently, the logic of your recommendation—the way you present your points—must make a good deal of sense to the reader. The burden of proof may tend to be heaviest on you, particularly if you are younger and less experienced than other personnel in the company.

This need not discourage you. Rather, it is to remind you that you should take a positive mental attitude toward your recommendations. It is also possible that your supervisor may have to report to someone above him. He may rely on the strength of the reasoning provided in your report to do some persuading of his own.

In a long, formal report one often must back up a series of recommendations with a good deal of data or information. Precisely how much data is supplied in a report will vary, of course, from report to report and from situation to situation. Nevertheless, even in a brief report, every word should be well-chosen, the facts well-outlined, and the recommendations should come as a logical outgrowth of the information in your report.

The assignment which follows will provide the student with some experience in the kind of thinking and writing that goes into a short report or memorandum in which recommendations are made.

Now do Assignment #10 on page 42

Communicating Information

Thus far we have talked about communicating ideas and recommendations in a report. Here we will talk about situations in which the supervisor is calling essentially for information. In order to appreciate the need to communicate information in a report, the reader might ask himself: *Why would my supervisor want an assemblage of knowledge, facts, or various data?*

There is probably no single answer to the question just asked. The supervisor may want information for any number of reasons: *planning, administration, organization or reorganization, control, or evaluation.* In other words, any of the basic functions of operations of business may require that he get fresh information in order to make a particular decision.

In marketing, for example, your sales manager may want information on a particular product. He may want to determine whether or not there is need for a price adjustment. He may want to make judgments regarding your effectiveness as a salesman. He may want to confer with research in marketing to determine whether or not a new or cheaper product should be made—whether a better product should be made, and so on. Control and evaluation of progress, as we have said before, necessitates that reports be provided and information communicated to supervisors.

To facilitate the communication of information many companies have routine report forms.

In fact, a considerable amount of information in industry is communicated routinely by report forms. Some examples of routine report forms are: *sales reports, financial reports, progress reports, personnel reports,* and *performance appraisal reports.*

These reports are designed to get certain information needed by a supervisor in the simplest, most effective way.

Some companies do not have a standard form, in which case a report would have to be written as a letter or as an original report.

The ability to encapsulate information and to record it precisely and concisely is appreciated very much in industry. Using routine forms can save time for both you and your supervisor, and provide a handy way of evaluating information for any number of purposes.

Now do Assignment #11 on page 43

Communicating Ability

The point has been made several times throughout the text, thus far, that report writing has many potential functions it can perform.

So far in this chapter, we have talked about the *communication of ideas, recommendations,* and *information.*

It also has been pointed out that reports are used as an indication of your own ability. There are instances in which you will be asked to write a report and be judged more for "how" you write a report than for "what" the report may say.

Occasionally, your supervisor may request a report specifically about you. When you are new with the company and when your current status or future potential in the company has not yet been adequately ascertained, reports can be used for such purposes.

A report can communicate much about your aptitude, intelligence, talent, and particular strengths. It may also communicate your weaknesses, your difficulties in understanding company business. Your work as a report writer will certainly say something about your ability to communicate.

Knowledge and Ability

Your knowledge of the workings of the company, your ability to make judgments, and your ability to communicate come across with the written word.

To help you do a better job as a report writer, the following checklist is supplied. Before sending out a report to be read by someone else, ask yourself these questions:

1. TO WHOM IS THE REPORT GOING?

2. WHAT IS THE VALUE AND PURPOSE OF THIS REPORT?

3. HAVE I MADE BY PURPOSE CLEAR?

4. IS MY MESSAGE WELL ORGANIZED?

5. HAVE I SPELLED EVERY WORD CORRECTLY?

6. HAVE I BEEN SHORT AND TO THE POINT?

7. AM I LETTING MY "EGO" SHINE THROUGH TOO MUCH?

8. AM I SPECIFIC AND DIRECT?

9. DOES MY REPORT HOLD TOGETHER AS AN INTELLIGENT, ORGANIZED, AND CONCISE PIECE OF BUSINESS COMMUNICATION?

Now do Assignment #12 on page 44

ASSIGNMENT #9

Instructions: In order to provide some experience in communicating ideas by way of a report, consider some situations where you work—part-time, full-time—at home, or at school. Consider some situation such as the following: parking, dining, studying, heating, or some other situation. Regardless of whether you are pleased with the situation or not, assume for the moment that the situation could be improved. There are few situations which cannot be improved in one way or another.

Before doing any writing, study the situation very carefully. Make some preliminary notes on the subject, and using your imagination, outline a series of suggestions which you think would improve the situation. However, leave it to the supervisor, or recipient of the report, to select the idea or suggestion which he thinks would best improve the situation. Your ideas could be the basis of a good discussion the next time the class meets.

This format will help you to organize your thinking:

TO: DATE:

FROM:

SUBJECT: _____

STATEMENT OF THE PROBLEM: _____

_____

_____

_____

HISTORY OF THE PROBLEM: _____

_____

_____

_____

_____

SUGGESTIONS: _____

_____

_____

_____

_____

_____

_____

ASSIGNMENT #10

Instructions: Assume that you have been requested to recommend new equipment for your company or school—equipment which would be helpful for the workers or students. Select an item—such as a typewriter, calculator, computer, photocopier—which you feel would be helpful in the office where you work or at school.

Do the background research for this report by way of actual communication with appropriate companies—by telephone, by letter of inquiry, or by personal visit.

After you have accumulated enough information, organize your material and prepare to write your report.

Use the form below to outline your report and accompanying recommendations.

TO: DATE:

FROM:

SUBJECT: _____

_____

1. Recommendation: _____

_____

_____

_____

2. Cost: _____

_____

_____

3. Possible Results: _____

_____

_____

_____

4. Benefits: _____

_____

_____

_____

_____

ASSIGNMENT #11

Instructions: Assume that you have been asked by your supervisor or professor to provide a report on a job, class, activity, trip, or conference which took place in connection with your studies or work.

Do the necessary research, organize your information, then think through the requirements of the report.

Use the form which follows to prepare the report. You do not need to write in complete sentences. You should, however, write or type neatly, and provide the basic facts on the information called for.

_____

TO: DATE:

FROM:

SUBJECT:

Name of Trip: _____

Place: _____

Purpose: _____

_____

_____

Results: _____

_____

_____

Cost: _____

_____

Comments: _____

_____

_____

_____

_____

_____

_____

ASSIGNMENT #12

Instructions: Assume that a new section of the company is being opened up. For this new section a supervisor is needed. You are desirous of getting this job as supervisor. Assume that it is a supervisory capacity which you could very well handle.

On the enclosed form enter the appropriate information on this report form which will qualify you for the job.

In order to fill out this report properly, it will probably be necessary that you do some research, thinking, and reviewing of your own background—and that you discuss the assignment with your classmates, your instructor, your relatives, and your friends.

The feedback which is likely to flow from such a discussion will help you to complete this assignment, and it can also be very helpful in planning your future.

On the form below enter the appropriate information which will qualify you for the job.

TO: _____   DATE:

FROM:

SUBJECT:

Job Objective: _____

_____

_____

Education or Training: _____

_____

_____

Comparable Experience: _____

_____

_____

Community or Social Experience Relating to Job: _____

_____

_____

Other Preparation for Job: _____

_____

_____

Original Ideas on Job: _____

_____

_____

CHAPTER 4

MAKING IT CLEAR AND COHERENT

In the last chapter, we talked about the purpose of a report. In this chapter we will talk about specific guidelines to the actual process of writing a report. The purpose of this chapter is to give you some guidelines which will help make your writing clear and coherent.

The responsible supervisor wants to be able to understand exactly what it is that you are saying. You need not impress him with a large vocabulary, especially with words which may lead to ambiguity. What is *not* wanted in business is writing which is muddy, writing which is unclear, or writing which leaves the receiver confused as to your intended meaning. *Clarity* and *coherence* should be the two goals toward which we strive.

There is no one way to accomplish clear, lucid writing. Expressing one idea at a time will help. Keeping your vocabulary simple and your sentences brief are two other ways in which you can work towards clarity.

"Coherence" means writing that holds together. "Coherence" is related to the word "cohesive," meaning a quality of sticking together. Your writing should "stick" or hold together. This can be accomplished in part by writing so that there is a natural and logical connection between your thoughts as expressed in your report.

The Essentials of Business Communication

The remarks above have emphasized the essential characteristics of good business communication: *clarity* and *coherence*. Business leaders want you to say what you mean and mean what you say. They want the ideas, information, and recommendations you are presenting in a business report, dressed in language they can understand. Now we will go beyond this brief introduction to the topics of this chapter and discuss various aspects of the use of language which contribute to effective report writing.

The Organization of the Sentence

General dictionary definitions of "the sentence" describe it as a grammatical unit of one or more words expressing a complete thought. Typically, a sentence is an independent statement, question, or request.

Realistically, when we take a look at language, as used, we know that an exclamation such as "Ouch!" can be appreciated to be a complete sentence. In a certain context this sentence says something complete.

Consider this question: "Where is he?" If the answer comes back: "Standing in the hallway," we cannot say that the answer is an incomplete sentence; it is a complete thought.

Such example sentences illustrate the fragmented nature of everyday communication. Yet we recognize that in some contexts they are quite complete instances of communication.

In report writing, it is best to hold on to a more formalized sentence structure. Because the sentence is a basic unit of communication, it is preferable to write a forthright sentence with a clear subject, predicate and object. It should be crystal clear "who" is doing "what" for "whom."

The modifiers—adjectives and adverbs, phrases and clauses—should be placed so as to effect the maximum amount of clarity. As a writer you can still endeavor to achieve a certain amount of variety; however, not at the expense of clear communication.

Now do Assignment #13 on page 51

Emphasis

We discover in writing, as in life, that all things are *not* equal. If everything were of equal importance, our communication would tend to come across to the reader as a blur.

If we think our ideas through intelligently, there is usually one point, one portion, one aspect of our report that is more important than the other parts. This should come across in our writing.

Emphasis is *stress* which is placed upon particular ideas. For example: "The supervisor's report gave special emphasis to the price." It is fairly obvious that the important idea in the sentence is *price*.

There are different ways in which emphasis can be achieved in writing. Repeating our ideas in the course of our writing is one way of achieving emphasis. Particular words or ideas can be stressed by the position in which they are located in the sentence. The end of a sentence is a good place for emphasis. This is called "periodic emphasis," as in the previous example in which "price" was stressed.

It is also possible to achieve emphasis by using *superlatives*, that is, words like "best" or "worst." In general, it is better to avoid extra devices for emphasis, such as underlining, putting in capital letters, or setting off phrases or words in quotation marks.

In formal report writing, emphasis is best achieved by the position in the writing which you give to important ideas. Sometimes it is a good idea to put the most important idea first.

For example, "Profits are what we are after."

The least helpful place to put a significant idea is the middle. *First* or *last* is the place for significant ideas.

Now do Assignment #14 on page 53

Parallel Construction

Parallel construction is another effective means of accomplishing *clarity* and *coherence.*

What is parallel structure? Parallel structure is the arrangement of phrases, sentences, or paragraphs in such a way as to suggest equality among the ideas expressed. For example: "With malice toward none; with charity for all; with firmness in the right . . ." This well-known quotation from Abraham Lincoln's "Second Inaugural Address" is an illustration of parallel structure.

The familiar "To err is human, to forgive divine" by Alexander Pope is another example of parallel structure.

The use of parallel structure lends clarity and force to one's writing.

Now do Assignment #15 on page 55

Organization of Paragraphs

A paragraph is a larger unit of communication in a written report. Paragraphs are identified by an indented first sentence, and by an extra line of spacing before and after them.

Paragraphing is a useful device for both the reader and the writer. It helps the writer subdivide his thoughts, and it conveys to the reader a separation between one unit of thought and another.

The following are some general thoughts and guidelines on the writing of effective paragraphs in reports:

1. Build your paragraph around one idea or topic.

    A paragraph consists of a major idea, often with some minor points or details which help develop and explain the paragraph.

2. Write your paragraph with a distinct "topic sentence."

    It is helpful to the reader to have one specific topic in the paragraph and one sentence for specifying that topic. This helps establish unity for each paragraph. It is a good idea to begin your paragraph with a topic sentence or close your paragraph with a topic sentence.

3. <u>Keep your paragraphs short</u>.

Too lengthy a paragraph becomes a block of grey to the reader; hence, one that is difficult to read. Although one main idea to a paragraph is a good principle to follow, the visual impact on the reader is an important consideration in deciding when next to paragraph.

Sometimes it is effective to write a one-sentence paragraph emphasizing one special idea. However, this should be done selectively.

Transitions

Transitions are words, phrases, or sentences which help the reader make the connection between one thought and another. Keep in mind the need for transitions between paragraphs. A paragraph does not generally exist by itself, especially in a report. Ordinarily, it represents the extension of ideas expressed earlier or leads into ideas which are forthcoming.

Transitions are an important device needed to pull one's writing together.

There are two basic ways of accomplishing transition. The first is the use of connectives—words which will facilitate the crossing over of one thought into another; and second, sentences which provide connecting ideas that help the reader to follow the development of your thoughts.

Consider the following sentence:

"There was a break in the water main that flooded the dormitory; therefore, the administration evacuated all the students."

The word *therefore* provides the connection between the ideas in the first sentence with ideas in the second.

The following is a list of words and phrases commonly used to achieve transition: *accordingly, afterward, consequently, furthermore, in addition, therefore, hence, however, since, finally, on the one hand,* and *on the other hand.*

The next time you write a memo, letter, or report, consider *transition.* Are there words or ideas which you can use to facilitate the connection of one idea with another?

Word Choice

How does one decide whether or not he has selected the best words with which to express himself? We have thousands upon thousands of words computerized in our minds; and yet we select certain words with which to express ourselves. Why do we select the words we do? There are a variety of explanations which linguists (those who study language scientifically) offer to explain our use of language.

Be that as it may, we ultimately decide upon certain words. To improve the quality of our word choice, there is much that we can learn from professional writers.

One difference between the professional writer and the average writer is that the professional is not easily satisfied with his word choices the first time he writes something.

The average person has a much larger command of the words in the English language than he gives himself credit for. From speaking, reading, and listening you probably have a richer reservoir of words than you realize.

To enhance your ability on word choice, ask yourself some of the following questions the next time you write:

1. ARE THE WORDS I HAVE CHOSEN CLEAR TO THE READER?

2. AM I BEING REPETITIOUS?

3. HAVE I USED A THESAURUS (*dictionary of synonyms*) TO HELP ME?

Now do Assignment #16 on page 57

ASSIGNMENT #13

Instructions: The sentences below are much less clearly written than they should be.

On the lines following each sentence, rewrite the sentence so that it is clear to the reader. Subjects, predicates, and modifiers should be placed so that there is no confusion as to the meaning of the sentence.

Interpret the sentence as you choose. But let that interpretation come across clearly to the reader. Feel free to rewrite the sentence as you see fit.

Ask your instructor to help if you have any difficulty understanding this assignment.

———————

1. The copy machine was shown to us by a representative whose monthly rental was $200.

   _____

   _____

   _____

2. We read about the kidnapped executive who was found in the *Wall Street Journal*.

   _____

   _____

   _____

3. The Vice President told us about entertaining an executive on the way out the door.

   _____

   _____

   _____

4. Our latest catalog we will send you because you asked for it.

   _____

   _____

   _____

5. For the position of secretary will be given careful consideration your application.

_____

_____

_____

6. How to arrange the conference room for the committee meeting the problem is for the supervisor.

_____

_____

_____

7. This product is the finest of its kind that may be if it is available.

_____

_____

_____

8. Uncertain that information was available he was not sure that the information was available.

_____

_____

_____

9. The president told us about seeing the latest in business skyscrapers and telecommunication satellites in the conference room.

_____

_____

_____

10. There were cartons of computer printouts provided by the Finance Department sent by the vice president of finance that were placed underneath the reception desk.

_____

_____

_____

ASSIGNMENT #14

Instructions: Rewrite the sentences which follow, giving emphasis to the word or phrase you consider most important.

Place the most important word or word group at or very near the end of the sentence. Also, arrange the words in order of their importance so as to secure a sense of suspense or building up of importance as you work toward the end of the sentence.

Feel free to edit or alter the sentences so as to make them easier to read.

1. Jack is an outstanding supervisor, he is a friend, and he is a congenial person.

   _____

   _____

   _____

2. We will reach the height of our sales promotion program, and first there will be a waiting period during which we will have to be patient and wait awhile.

   _____

   _____

   _____

3. There were a number of important people at the meeting: the president, the vice president, the supervisor, and the line foreman.

   _____

   _____

   _____

4. Cassette recorders are available at a number of price levels they sell for: as high as $300, $35, $50, $75, and $100.

   _____

   _____

   _____

5. When the staff received the report, the members were absolutely shocked when they came to the conclusion, it took them awhile to understand its meaning and what it all signified.

_____

_____

_____

6. The Board of Directors made several surprising changes in the company: they removed the president of the company, they removed the plant superintendent, and finally, they transferred my supervisor.

_____

_____

_____

7. The members of the union decided to go on strike—then they broke down, negotiation began congenially, and they were deadlocked for a period.

_____

_____

_____

8. The executive said that we would have a full week off for the holidays, that some minor changes would be made in production schedules, and that he was pleased to see us.

_____

_____

_____

ASSIGNMENT #15

Instructions: Rewrite the sentences below and convert them into structures that are parallel.

Rewrite the sentence by either altering the pattern of the first part of the sentence to run similar to that of the second; or the reverse; that is, alter or change the arrangement of words in the second part to agree with the first.

For example: Original sentence — "He was a strong leader who got us to follow him, and his voice was soft but you heard him."

Parallel structure — "He was a strong leader and got us to follow him; he was soft-spoken and got us to listen to him."

1. This accounting report is very well prepared; the person who prepared it arranged the material in easy-to-read fashion.

2. My supervisor spends his time working at his desk, looking around the office, or else he complains about the inefficient work habits of everyone else in the office.

3. Professors teaching in universities receive lower salaries; whereas, a professor who goes out into the business world can make considerably more, and sometimes the hours are less.

4. We gathered data about competitive products in the field, information was also gathered about the virtues of computers, what they were supposed to do as we found them in trade journals, and they also asked other people what their experience was with them.

55

5. The experience on the job improved my ability as a professional, and they noticed that I carried myself with more confidence.

_____

_____

_____

6. The customer turned out to be difficult to reach, uninterested, and also it seemed that he did not have a sense of humor.

_____

_____

_____

7. He said there was danger that the machine might jam; we also heard him say that the mechanical difficulties were being overcome.

_____

_____

_____

8. There were many professional opportunities which were open to us working in New York; also, there were lots of things you could do socially if you wanted to.

_____

_____

_____

9. Some people say that college training will prepare you to succeed in the business world; I have heard them say that you can also make it on your own.

_____

_____

_____

10. Our attendance will be required at the next business meeting; you will probably be put on notice if you work here and you don't go to the meeting.

_____

_____

_____

ASSIGNMENT #16

Instructions: Rewrite the sentences below. Keep in mind the discussion developed in this chapter on "word choice."

Use your dictionary, your thesaurus, your knowledge, and your imagination to rework these sentences.

1. A special newsreport on jobs was sent out to people on their jobs in offices and factories.

2. Confidence in the ability of the supervisor to do his job was fading because people thought his ability was not up to the job.

3. Nobody offered any good ideas on how to cut back on office spending because they didn't seem to have any ideas.

4. Our company is a place where changes come about slowly, if they do change at all.

5. Economic solutions for the state and federal government are not always developed out of the best economic principles.

6. On the topic of fashions, many companies are more liberal in the fashions they allow in their company.

_____

_____

_____

7. On-the-job training provides for effective training for a job.

_____

_____

_____

8. Those who wish to manage a large company must be ready for the pressure and frustration that go along with high-pressure jobs in a large company.

_____

_____

_____

9. For its employees, the airline company provided substantial pay increases for its employees who were involved in the strike, as well as those who were not.

_____

_____

_____

10. Job safety was finally given more attention for those who had originally requested it in the committee dedicated to achieving job safety.

_____

_____

_____

CHAPTER 5
WRITING CORRECTLY

In a day and age in which there is so much change, it is difficult, if not impossible, to assert that certain rules or guidelines are the correct ones. This constant change makes it impossible to state anything in absolute terms. How many of us can formulate a statement which will be absolutely true for all times and all people? Such an assignment is just about impossible.

A more fitting title for this chapter might be "Writing Appropriately." And—writing appropriately is a proper consideration for our book.

Granted, there is a great deal of change today. Still it can be said that certain things are correct or incorrect; appropriate or inappropriate. In this sense, the word *correct* can still be used with a good deal of authority, if not absolutely.

For example, it seems appropriate that there be some sort of formal or "Sunday dress" for a wedding. Somehow dirty jeans, sneakers, and a torn tee-shirt do not seem appropriate for a formal occasion. A special occasion calls for a certain amount of formality for even the most liberal thinkers. So, too, in writing we realize that a certain amount of formality and standardization is appropriate from time to time.

Standards in Usage

On usage, then, the best lead is *appropriateness*. When in doubt as to whether to be formal or informal with word patterns, think of the following basic rhetorical considerations: the *writer*, the *subject*, the *audience*.

First, what is most comfortable for you, the writer? Saying: "Each should use *his* own equipment" may or may not set well with you. You may prefer to say: "Each should use *their* own equipment."

The formal agreement pattern of "each" with "his" fits in with the formal report writing pattern; the informal pattern of "each" with "their" fits in with the informal setting.

Second, the topic of the report itself may imply certain language choices. If, for instance, the topic is related to a formal business recommendation, a formal set of usage patterns will be preferable. Formal patterns may help make clear and strengthen what is being communicated. If the topic has to do with a company or class Christmas party or outing, so-called correct usage patterns may detract from the lightness and informality which the writer may want to convey.

Third, the reading audience should be analyzed. A liberal college classroom or an informal "rap" session may suggest one set of language choices—the informal patterns. A formal business conference at the executive level may suggest another—the formal patterns.

It is not within the province of this text to include all the possible guides to correctness for which to be alert. Samuel Johnson said: "Knowledge is of two kinds: we know a subject ourselves, or we know where we can find information upon it." A good place for the student to begin, then, is with some basic reference material. The following list of references is basic:

1. A GOOD COLLEGIATE DESK DICTIONARY

2. A THESAURUS OF SYNONYMS

3. A HANDBOOK OF CORRECT ENGLISH USAGE

As we have said, it is important to have references which will help you on the subjects of meaning, variety, and correct or appropriate usage. Money invested in such basic references will pay you dividends when you are hard at work writing and need help.

In the confines of this chapter, we will provide practice on a few basic areas which will assist you in eliminating some of the more common errors which crop up in business writing.

It should be noted that the work on usage in this chapter should be viewed only as a beginning. An exhaustive workout on all kinds of errors would not be efficient, since not all of us make the same kinds of mistakes in writing.

Rule 1: Write with a Strong Sense of Subject and Predicate

The difference between formal and informal usage with respect to the sentence has already been discussed. The need to write with a subject and predicate in report writing has also been emphasized.

Now do Assignment #17 on page 66

Rule 2: Make Sure that the Subject and Predicate Agree in Number

Grammatical agreement has to do with correspondence in number of the subject and the predicate. *A singular subject takes a singular verb.*

Examples: Singular — "He hits the ball."

Plural — "They hit the ball."

Sometimes it is helpful to think of the *s* in the verb. In this case, *hit* carries an *s* . . . indicating the singular form of the verb.

Now do Assignment #18 on page 68

Rule 3: Certain Indefinite Pronouns Take a Singular Verb

The following commonly used pronouns are singular and take a singular verb: *each, either, neither, one, everyone, everybody, no one, nobody, anyone, anybody, someone,* and *somebody.*

Frequently, these words are followed by phrases that may contain plural terms. However, the determination is based on subject and verb agreement, not with the words in any intervening phrase.

For example: "Each of the secretaries is willing to do her part."

Notice that "each" is singular and that the verb "is" is singular. Notice, too, that the intervening prepositional phrase "of the secretaries" does not affect the agreement of subject and verb.

Now do Assignment #19 on page 70

Rule 4: A Pronoun Should Agree With Its Antecedent in Number and Gender

A *pronoun* is a word that takes the place of a noun. An *antecedent* is a word which precedes or goes before a pronoun. It is the noun to which the pronoun refers.

For example: "Each man brought his own copy of the agenda."

Notice that the "his" refers back to "man." The pronoun and antecedent agree in number and gender. In the above illustration "his" agrees with "man" both in number and gender. *Gender* indicates whether it is *male* or *female.*

The assignment which follows will give you practice in checking on the agreement between *pronoun* and *antecedent.*

Now do Assignment #20 on page 72

A Continuous Job

Writing correctly is not something one learns once and accomplishes for all time. Undoubtedly, you have had some instruction and experience in writing and the correct way to write.

The principles introduced in this chapter will serve as a refresher for you, but this is only part of the job.

There are many points regarding the use of subjects, verbs, pronouns, modifiers, phrases, clauses, and sentence structure that you may want to look up as you take a closer and more careful look at the way you write—particularly the way you write reports.

A Guide to Spelling

Spelling is a topic that has consumed the time and energy of many people. History tells us that Andrew Jackson, seventh president of the United States, never spelled very well and is renowned for having said the following: "It is a darn poor mind that can think of only one way to spell a word!" It is recorded that the author of *The Great Gatsby*—F. Scott Fitzgerald—was a particularly poor speller. Theodore Roosevelt was so concerned about the problem of spelling that he tried to pass legislation which would simplify spelling and put it on a closer relationship with the way words are sounded.

Perhaps you heard the story of the two secretaries comparing bosses, and one said her boss was bigoted.

The other said: "Bigoted? How come?"

The first one said: "Well, he thinks words can be spelled in only one way."

A Guide to Improved Spelling

One place to begin, in considering how to improve spelling, is the way you speak. It may be that you are saying some words incorrectly and are, as a result, spelling them wrong.

For example, if you pronounce the word *idea* as "ideaR," you may very well add an "r" to the word when you spell it. If you pronounce the word *February*, the month that comes after January, as "Febuary," don't be surprised if you leave out the "r" when you spell it. Misspelling words such as *libary* for "library," *goverment* for "government," and others, may come from too casual an approach to pronunciation.

Guidelines to the Improvement of Spelling

1. Start a spelling list of just those words which you have a tendency to misspell.

2. Regularly go over your list prior to the writing of a report.

3. Regularly use your dictionary.

4. Review rules for correct spelling.

Spelling Rules and Rhymes

In order to spell *some* words correctly, one must memorize the correct spelling. Unfortunately, there are no short cuts in those cases. On the other hand, not all words must be memorized individually.

There are many words that conform to definite patterns. Perhaps the most familiar is the *ie* pattern.

63

You may remember the old rhyme:

"*i* before *e*, except after *c*, or when sounded as "ay" as in *neighbor* and *weigh*."

Many words, indeed, do conform to this pattern. For instance: *receive*, *believe*, *chief*, and *ceiling*. There are other patterns with which one can familiarize himself. However, that will require a little more detailed presentation than we have space for in this chapter.

Anyone having particular problems with spelling should make an attempt to follow some of the guidelines provided in this section on spelling. If spelling is, indeed, a problem, get a book which specializes in the difficulties of spelling.

Revision

To give yourself the best opportunity to produce an effective report, do not concentrate on such tasks as editing and proofreading the first time through. In the first draft, concentrate on the flow of ideas.

Then, after completing a first draft, sit back and carefully and critically appraise what you have written. Do not allow yourself to jump into a final draft copying your work exactly as it appears the first time. Matters such as those that have been studied in this chapter should be contemplated: *standards of usage, correctness*, and *spelling*.

Also, one should check for *clarity and coherence*, going over such matters as have been covered in Chapter Four: *organization of sentences, organization of paragraphs, emphasis, parallel construction, transitions*, and *word choice*.

Upon completing your critical evaluation of the first draft, it is advisable to put the draft aside. If you set aside the report for a while and return to it another hour or day, your materials will take on a new look, and you will probably be in a better frame of mind—fresh with new energy—to apply some of your own constructive criticism.

A good practice in writing is to attempt the initial draft at the earliest possible date, so that you will have time before any "due date" to revise and improve your work.

Proofreading

A countless number of businessmen learn too late that it is a mistake to pass on all responsibilities to a secretary. Such a practice simply does not work. The individual responsible is the individual who hands in the report, regardless of whether or not he or she did the final typewriting on the draft. Many a secretary is highly skilled and responsible. Just as many are not. How can you be sure?

Consequently, the responsibility for careful proofreading falls upon the writer—the individual who delivers or hands in the report.

Remember, too, that any typist is only human. She is capable of error as well as you. Neither can you rely solely on her for perfection in wording, punctuation, or spelling.

Sometimes obvious errors in numbering and spelling make both the writer and the typist look foolish.

Proofreading must be done slowly and carefully. The tendency for most of us, particularly when we are familiar with the contents of a composition or a report, is to want to skim along at a high speed. Proofreading demands slow and careful reading. As with revision, proofreading is done best after an interval of time—an hour or two, or a day or two, depending on what the given schedule will allow.

In any event, remember that proofreading—detecting and correcting any errors that remain in the final draft of a report—is a responsibility that falls upon you. For yours is the name "on the bottom line" and errors that remain in the report reflect, not on your typewriting assistant, but on you.

ASSIGNMENT #17

Instructions: The sentences below are lacking either a complete subject or predicate. They are, therefore, considered incomplete sentences in formal writing.

For example: Incomplete Sentence — Placed the sales reports in their proper place.

     Complete Sentence — She placed the sales reports in their proper place.

On the lines below, rewrite the sentences and add the subject or predicate needed. You may want to do a rough draft of your sentence on scrap paper before entering your corrected sentence on the blanks below.

––––––––––––

1. Uncovering the work of an untrained artist a lot of looking.

––

––

2. Was indicted for allegedly mishandling the company funds.

––

––

3. The panel's appearance before the entire business group entertaining as it was.

––

––

––

4. The new administration in an effort to hold back expenses.

––

––

5. Construction of the new plant although expected to begin right away.

––

––

6. Wiser to retrain present employees.

––

––

7. Because of the rising cost of living, transferring employees.

   _____

   _____

8. Liked the car pools as an opportunity to save money and to meet new people.

   _____

   _____

9. That international peace would help business as well.

   _____

   _____

10. Died at an early age due the stress on him, in a hectic career in the music business.

    _____

    _____

ASSIGNMENT #18

Instructions: The sentences below do not agree in number—the subjects and verbs are out of line— one is singular and the other plural, or the other way around.

For example: Incorrect Sentence — The vice presidents is all leaving.

             Correct Sentence   — The vice presidents are all leaving.

On the lines below rewrite the sentences and correct the subject or verb in number. You may want to do a rough draft on scrap paper before entering your corrected version on the lines below.

1. The new president follow the former one's style of administration.

2. He were very much excited about trying out the new company car.

3. The insurance coverage seem adequate for the amount of assets contained within the building.

4. Increased powers is given to the executive secretary who prove her capabilities.

5. A motor bike can prove to be fun and good exercise on country roads but are likely to be dangerous on downtown city streets.

6. Since he is one who appreciates the theater, he go whenever he can.

7. The electric company are under a great deal of criticism due to a hike in prices.

_____

_____

8. More and more business machines is being advertised in newspapers and magazines.

_____

_____

9. The building are more than adequate for the many seminars, conferences, and meetings scheduled in it.

_____

_____

10. Many people wish that trolley cars would comes back.

_____

_____

ASSIGNMENT #19

Instructions: The sentences below are not correct in agreement—the subject and verb do not correspond in number. Either the subject is plural and the verb is singular, or the subject is singular and the verb is plural.

For example: Incorrect Sentence — Everyone who works in this office try to do their very best.

           Correct Sentence   — Everyone who works in this office tries to do his very best.

On the lines below rewrite the sentences and correct the subject or the verb as required. You may want to do a rough draft of your sentence on scrap paper before entering your corrected version on the blanks below.

---

1. Each of the speakers have demonstrated a good control of his subject matter.

   _____

   _____

2. Somebody in the office were singing softly to himself.

   _____

   _____

3. We weren't surprised at the robbery; not one of the doors are ever locked.

   _____

   _____

4. Everyone in the department take a coffee break at the same time.

   _____

   _____

5. Do your supervisor want a cup of coffee?

   _____

   _____

6. Nobody in my section have ever used this kind of equipment before.

   _____

   _____

7. Everybody in the company have been talking about the company party Saturday night.

_____

_____

8. One of the reports were already completed.

_____

_____

9. Everyone in the company were very much impressed with the new benefits announced by the personnel department.

_____

_____

10. Someone in that group of accountants are responsible for a tax summary and forecast.

_____

_____

ASSIGNMENT #20

Instructions: In the sentences below, the pronouns do not agree with their antecedents. The sentences are, therefore, incorrect.

For example: Incorrect Sentence — Each of the managers looked happy because they had pleased the president.

Correct Sentence — Each of the managers looked happy because he had pleased the president.

On the lines below, rewrite and correct the sentences on agreement. You may want to do a rough draft of your sentence on scrap paper before entering your corrected version on the blanks.

———————

1. When George sees someone that he knows he invariably pauses and talks to them.

    ————————————————————————————————

    ————————————————————————————————

2. Jack or Al will lend us their copy of the annual report.

    ————————————————————————————————

    ————————————————————————————————

3. Each of the girls displayed their certificate for the training course.

    ————————————————————————————————

    ————————————————————————————————

4. Neither supervisor took the time to apologize for their mistakes.

    ————————————————————————————————

    ————————————————————————————————

5. In view of the fine record of community service, each member should be proud of their company.

    ————————————————————————————————

    ————————————————————————————————

6. Each of the boys brought their own lunch.

_____

_____

7. Each of the employees ran to the window nearest their desk.

_____

_____

8. One of the workers lost their cool.

_____

_____

9. Jack and Gerry has their work ready on time. (Present tense)

_____

_____

10. Several of the workers refused to eat his food until the job was done.

_____

_____

CHAPTER 6

WRITING TO BE READ

Thus far, we have been talking about and working on the problems of writing from the *writer's* point of view. We have also been talking about the kinds of topics or problems one actually encounters in the business world.

We have not as yet talked with precision about the reading audience; that is to say, the *receiver* in the communication process.

Therefore, it is appropriate that we give some consideration to the problems of the reader as he perceives the report we are writing. It is important that we observe standards and that we know the subject matter of our report. If we are to be successful in our communication efforts, it is equally important to give consideration to the problems of the reader. To complete the communication process, the reader must be able to understand the writer. Further, it is significant that the reader be comfortable as well. The reader may be trapped into reading. In order to keep his job, he may have to read what you have written. However, if you consider him while you are preparing your materials, and anticipate the problems of reading properly, you can make it easier for him to read your report—and leave a positive impression of your ability as a writer. By keeping certain guidelines in mind, therefore, we can avoid having the reader of our reports suffer throughout our material, misunderstand it, or in other ways do an injustice to our efforts to come up with a good report. Our goal as a writer should be to capture the interest of the reader at the beginning of the report and keep it throughout.

It is helpful to have a human relations understanding of those for whom we are writing, but here we will simply consider guidelines to better writing.

We will now work on the following principles of good report writing: *writing on the reader's level, being concise, avoiding clichés, pacing yourself, keeping your tone appropriate,* and *being specific.*

Writing on the Reader's Level

To be sure that your reader understands what is being said, evaluate him somewhat as follows:

First, are you writing a report for someone within your company? If the individual for whom you are writing works in the same company that you do, you may assume that he has some appreciation of the kind of business operation of which you are both a part.

Second, in what function of the business operation does your reader work? If you are writing for an immediate supervisor, you may safely assume that he knows the nature of the business you are writing about, so that you may use language with which he is familiar. Commonly, you will be writing about problems with which you are both concerned.

On the other hand, it is possible that you are researching some subject with which he is not familiar and you are bringing new information into your division and the company. If this is the case, you are going to have to be explicit, clear, and you must define any new terms which you are including in your report.

If you are writing horizontally in the company—to someone who works at a different function in the company—you will have to keep in mind that your reader may not entirely understand the workings and the language of your work-a-day problems.

If, for example, you are in the marketing division and are concerned with sales, certain words, expressions, and concepts which *you* use every day of the week may be completely unfamiliar to those in the Accounting Department. And, of course, the reverse would be true—accountants do not necessarily use or understand the language of sales. As a result, it is necessary that we keep in mind the specialization and differences of language as we use it in business today.

In short, we must consider the audience we are writing for in terms of the following: *area of general interest, specialization,* and *educational level.*

Being Concise

The ability to cover a subject adequately with a few words is greatly respected in business. Being brief, yet comprehensive, will build a good reputation for you in both oral and written communication. That man who can provide a quick and concise explanation of the business at hand is sought after.

"Brevity is the soul of wit," said Shakespeare. You will find that this one quote is widely known by businessmen and, again, *greatly appreciated.*

Time is of the essence; time is money in business. Supervisors, customers, anyone you will be writing for wants to understand what you are saying in the fewest number of words possible, as long as you *don't sacrifice accuracy for brevity.* Your report should be long enough to cover the subject but short enough to be read and correctly understood. Assignment #21 is designed to give you practice in the art of being concise.

Now do Assignment #21 on page 79

Avoiding Clichés

One way of approaching the problem of effective report writing is to concentrate on keeping the reader's attention and helping him understand us by being concise. We have talked about this and have practiced this in the above assignment.

Another way of enhancing our report writing so that it will, in fact, be read is to *avoid clichés.*

A *cliché* is a *stereotype expression*. Eliminating clichés from your writing will help you write more directly and honestly for the benefit of your reader.

Now do Assignment #22 on page 82

Trite, Worn-out Phrases

A trite phrase is one which lacks freshness because it is used excessively. Changing or editing one's writing in order to avoid clichés can sometimes be an obvious process. However, the newcomer to good business communication will need to take some time in order to discover which are "trite and worn-out phrases."

The material which follows is offered as an introduction to assist the writer in familiarizing himself or herself with some of the expressions which are over-used in business communication.

Trite Phrases to Avoid

1. ALONG THIS LINE
2. AND THINGS LIKE THAT
3. AT YOUR EARLIEST CONVENIENCE
4. DOOMED TO DISAPPOINTMENT
5. FIRST AND FOREMOST
6. GET OUR WIRES CROSSED
7. GOES WITHOUT SAYING
8. IF I HAD IT TO DO OVER AGAIN
9. IN THE FINAL ANALYSIS
10. NONE THE WORSE FOR WEAR

A list of trite and worn-out phrases ultimately ends up being an arbitrary matter. A comparison of lists of phrases which one writer considers trite and worn-out will not necessarily agree with a list that another writer calls trite and worn-out. It all depends on what one has heard and read.

Nevertheless, one should be on the lookout for those phrases and expressions which are, in the writer's experience, overused. Sensitivity to this aspect of writing will keep the writer on his toes and will encourage him to make every effort to be fresh and interesting in the way he expresses himself.

Pacing Yourself

Pacing has to do with the rate of movement. Ordinarily, one would expect to apply the word to walking, hiking, or running. But the expression "pacing" can be applied to the writing and reading of reports as well as other activities. The point here is that though the report may seem to us to move along, we must assist the reader by helping him measure off what he is reading. Try to avoid giving your reader too much too soon. By identifying the various sections of your report, you can help him pace himself and enhance your ability to get your message across.

As we know from driving on turnpikes and superhighways, we tend to pace ourselves by following the signs we find along the highway. One way to insure that your written report will reach the mark is to give the reader signs to follow, too.

Work on the topography of your report. The topography has to do with the outline or shape of your report. The visual impact the report will make on your reader is an important consideration.

Avoid having your report come across to the reader as a "block of grey," which may discourage him from reading the report. If he does read it, he may literally have to grit his teeth, and plow through the message or data.

The following are some suggestions to help you "pace" your writing. These devices will help your reader to pace his reading.

1. *USE SIMPLE WORDS.*

    One or two long words (of three or more syllables) are enough in a sentence.

2. *USE SHORT SENTENCES.*

    Hold the average to twenty words or under per sentence.

3. *USE REGULAR PHRASES.*

    Pause at the end / of a complete unit of thought / before going to another unit of thought.

4. *USE BRIEF PARAGRAPHS.*

    Short paragraphs are easier and more restful for tired eyes to read.

5. *USE VISUAL AIDS.*

    It is a simple truth of communication that a picture is worth many words.

We will take up the topic of visual aids in greater detail later on in the text. For this reason, treatment of the topic here will be brief. It is sufficient to say that any visual aids that you can include with your writing will help you pace your writing and facilitate the reading of the report. Such devices as under-lining, double and triple spacing, indenting, alphabetizing, numbering, and others will serve to break up the material and highlight the points you are making.

ASSIGNMENT #21

Instructions: The sentences below are quite the opposite of being concise. They are long-winded and filled with unnecessary words.

These sentences can be edited without losing their essential meaning by *deleting* or *omitting* the unnecessary words.

Rewrite each of the sentences below on the spaces provided beneath them and demonstrate your ability to be concise. You may want to work out a rought draft of your edited and condensed version of the sentence before entering it in the blanks below.

1. It would appear that the executive board has given some attention to its implementation of equal rights in personnel policies or apparently this was the drift of what the executive board appeared to be talking about.

    _____

    _____

    _____

2. Business loans at many leading New York City banks have given the appearance of dropping in volume in recent weeks due to a decline which more or less resulted from inflationary pressures or so it seemed to be.

    _____

    _____

    _____

3. Rising prices, which are constantly going up during an inflationary period, require some sort of governmental action which demonstrates that the government is interested in achieving some sort of governmental participation and regulatory efforts on its part.

    _____

    _____

    _____

4. Those interested in ecology or the environment are very much and probably very often concerned about clean air and what the automobile leaders in that industry are doing to improve the environment.

    _____

    _____

    _____

5. It is not always easy and sometimes it is difficult, if not impossible, to determine the place of unions in business and whether or not unions are effective in improving the welfare of a company or not.

_____

_____

_____

6. The emphasis and stress or concern and interest in the preservation of energy is very much on the minds of people who are disturbed about the excessive use of energy by some, and the climbing prices of oil and other energy sources.

_____

_____

_____

7. It seems that the position or power or strength of the Arab oil producing countries has moved or shifted toward a position of strength in recent years.

_____

_____

_____

8. The amount of concern in space travel wavers from time to time, but the exploration goes on and on although expenditures of money for space travel do not always seem to be a priority in which there is an amount of concern.

_____

_____

_____

9. Office space for many of the executives in our company is not what some of the executives feel or want or not entirely as much as would provide them space in which to perform as efficiently as they might have if they have more space in which to work.

_____

_____

_____

10. The attitudes of many people towards politics have undergone many changes as their attitudes have changed in regard to politics.

_____

_____

_____

ASSIGNMENT #22

Instructions: Rewrite the sentences below, eliminating the cliché. To make it easy for you to identify the cliché in each sentence, it has been set off with quotation marks.

1. The supervisor moved the materials and files from his office "bag and baggage."

_____

_____

_____

2. One thing that could be said about his secretary was that she was "slow but sure."

_____

_____

_____

3. Working in the stockroom Mr. Jones felt that he had pretty much "led a dog's life."

_____

_____

_____

4. Though the company was in financial trouble, the president, Mr. Gold, felt that he should not "leave a sinking ship."

_____

_____

_____

5. One could always be sure that Jack would conduct a meeting coming in "fit as a fiddle."

_____

_____

_____

6. The complaint that many customers expressed to our salesman was that some of the merchandise was "as old as the hills."

_____

_____

_____

7. After all the difficulties we have had with the Accounting Department, yelling at the chief accountant was only to "add insult to injury."

_____

_____

_____

8. Working for such a difficult individual as our client in New Haven appeared to many to have been a "fate worse than death."

_____

_____

_____

9. Doing research for this particular report had to be very thorough—I was instructed to "leave no stone unturned."

_____

_____

_____

10. Waiting endlessly, as our company was forced to do, we finally received the merchandise "with open arms."

_____

_____

_____

CHAPTER 7
RESEARCHING
YOUR
INFORMATION

The value of research to industry has been proven beyond a doubt. It is generally recognized today that research is basic to business, as long as business wishes to be prosperous. Organizations can no longer afford to do what comes naturally in the stream of time; for without adequate research the organization may be racing headlong into disaster.

Consequently, as was pointed out earlier in the text, report writing—and the research that so often goes into report writing—holds a respected place in business.

The copious number of scientists working in industry is not an accident. Not only in the laboratory but throughout industry, we find the scientist as well as scientific methods in the various functions of the company—*administration, production, finance,* and *marketing.*

As we pointed out in the early chapters of the text, report writing is necessary for intelligent decision making. Research, whether modest or extensive, is typically the area in which long business reports are written.

Reports do not magically appear out of the sky, of course. Producing them requires the command of writing *and* research skills. The writer addresses himself to a particular problem. He marshals his facts to support his findings, and then he arranges them so that they are easily read. It is not within the province of this text to attempt every kind of research problem that businessmen need to have solved. Rather, it is to acquaint the student with the basic approaches needed in order to write a report; where the writing of the report may be more comprehensive, this text will point the student to guides, resources, and a variety of approaches he may need.

Defining Your Problem

It is one thing to sense directly or indirectly that there is a problem in a business situation. It is quite another to be able to define the problem with clarity. The ability to describe concisely and clearly what the problem is in a given situation is an ability which will mark the new businessman or business student as one with potential—one who can grow and be successful in business. The ability to define the problem is one that is well valued by supervisors and top managers.

So then, defining the problem, not with vague thinking or indefinite terms, but with clear thinking and exact terms is the challenge we will take up now.

Your job in approaching the problem is to establish its limits or boundaries. Limiting is part of defining the problem. Making definite the extent of the problem is a good way to begin. A good way of going about this is to formulate a statement.

A careful selection of words, phrases, or sentences should be used to specify the nature and extent of the problem. This is the first step one must take before proceeding with any research. The method that will be used will be determined to some extent by the way in which you state the problem.

Suppose a supervisor came to you complaining about the fact that the company telephone bill had doubled in the last two months. Since this was a bill which amounted to thousands of dollars, he felt it was no small matter. He wanted it investigated.

In general terms, the problem was this: *The supervisor wants to know why the telephone bill is so high.* Before you could do any work, there would have to be some thinking on the subject. We have a problem, and we might consider some of the possible causes: New personnel in the company? Carelessness of old personnel? New company affiliates? International business? All of these are possible causes that may enter into defining the problem. Each of these problem areas may, in turn, have to be subdivided before one can come to grips with the immediate cause of the problem: *an inexplicably high telephone bill.* There may be subdivision upon subdivision. A good deal of thinking and "spade work" (or digging into the problem) may be necessary.

After zeroing in on the problem, it could very well turn out that the items mentioned as possible causes may all revert to a larger problem of which you, as the new employee or as the supervisor, may not have been aware.

In business, for example, the doubling of an expense such as the telephone bill could have resulted from a policy which emanated from the top management of the company. Top management may have decided that the company should expand and move out. In keeping with this objective, the expanded amount of telephone communication may be completely justified, and may come as a natural consequence of an expanded business operation. Were this your finding, your report would shed some light on the realities of the company's position at the time of your report.

One has to approach a problem situation with a positive attitude. The best way to do that is to follow through systematically by beginning with a clear and concise statement of the problem. Once you have stated the problem clearly and concisely, you have a place to begin. You can discuss your statement of the problem with your supervisor or other members of the firm, and get some response as to whether or not you are on the right track. Once you get some feedback as to whether or not you have, indeed, stated the problem clearly, you can proceed either to rewrite the statement of the problem, defining it more precisely or in different terms than you had before, or proceed with your research.

When, indeed, you have assessed the problem properly—know the extent of it—you are ready to begin digging up the facts.

Now do Assignment #23 on page 92

Getting The Facts

Let us assume now that you have clearly and concisely stated the problem. Further, you have checked with your supervisor or someone who can act as an intelligent sounding board, to help you sharpen up and test out your statement of the problem.

It is time now for you to begin research on your problem. There are two basic ways of getting facts: *Library Research* and *Field Research*.

Library Research

Library Research will allow you to avail yourself of that information which is already gathered, information that is in resource form. Resource material may be in existence in company files. Another possibility is library resources. There may be pamphlets, periodicals, and books that may have all or parts of the information you may be seeking for your business research and the report which you have to prepare.

Library References

The references listed here will give the student an idea where in the library to get information on the business world.

1. **Business Periodicals Index:** This is the reference source to look into for magazine articles regarding business areas.

2. **Applied Science and Technology Index:** This reference will help you to locate articles of a scientific and technical nature.

3. **Readers' Guide to Periodical Literature:** This is the library tool for general magazine articles.

4. **The New York Times Index:** In this reference one can find any news item that appeared in the *Times*.

5. **Poor's Register of Directors and Executives:** This reference provides data regarding business connections, addresses, dates and places of birth for more than 80,000 top management people.

6. **Who's Who in America:** Perhaps the most used library tool with information on living persons.

Other references of interest are *Current Biography; Information Please Almanac; World Almanac; Subject Guide to Books in Print; Biography Index; Hammond's World Atlas; Rand McNally's Cosmopolitan World Atlas; A Popular Guide to Government Publications; Selected U.S. Government Publications;* and any other good multi-volume encyclopedia.

Which References

Your selection of a library reference will depend on what you are looking for. Before selecting one of the many resources available, give some thought to the following questions:

1. ABOUT WHAT OR WHOM ARE YOU LOOKING FOR INFORMATION?

2. WHAT ARE SOME SIGNIFICANT DATES CONNECTED WITH THE PERSON, PLACE, THINGS OR IDEAS YOU ARE RESEARCHING?

3. HOW EXTENSIVE IS THE INFORMATION YOU NEED?

Your answers to these questions will help you zero in on the appropriate references for your research project.

In addition to the above, the student should be aware that there are other financial and industrial directories, and statistical references which could, in one form or another, contain some of the facts that the researcher may be seeking. Consequently, there would be no need for the student to duplicate what is already in existence.

Gathering Your Information First-hand

The previous discussion has to do with facts or data which are already available in existing libraries, or in reports in company files. Once the student or businessman has thoroughly satisfied himself that *no* information *has been gathered* on the stated problem, then the researcher is faced with the problem of gathering his own information.

Primary Sources

It well may be that you have already had experience in gathering information for research—possibly without being aware of it. For instance, you may (under the heading of politics) have gone about the neighborhood to find out political preferences in an impending election. In such cases, *you* gathered the information from the primary source itself. The way in which you assembled the material and reported on it resembles very much the kind of thing one does in business research.

Methods of Research

Research is the systematic inquiry or investigation into a subject in order to discover new knowledge or evaluate ideas. Business research goes into such areas as *economics, human relations, markets,* and *marketing.*

There are basic methods employed in research.

It should be noted that the following commentary is a simplification of research methods, but it will serve to give the reader an overview of the basic approaches to research.

- *The Historical Method:* In this method, the researcher attempts to discover the past or present experience of people or companies with a product, method, or idea.

- *The Statistical Method:* In this method, the process involves collecting data as to how many of a certain product, method, or idea are in use or existence.

- *The Survey Method:* In this method, the attempt is to find out to what extent people like a given person, place, thing, or idea.

- *The Laboratory Method:* In this method, the attempt is to test the potential of a product, method, or idea through experimentation.

The Survey Method

The survey method is a useful way of learning what people think about current problems, methods, things, or ideas. It is somewhat synonymous with the poll of public opinion with which most of us are familiar. The method consists of asking a number of people how they feel about something. If this number is properly selected, the survey can be a useful gauge to public opinion. The method is sometimes called "sampling."

In evaluating and analyzing the results of your survey, do not overgeneralize on your findings. The results of your survey have limitations which will depend on such factors as: *age, educational background, geographical location, income, social class,* and so on.

The basic steps to conducting a reliable survey are as follows:

1. DEFINE THE OBJECTIVES.

2. FORMULATE THE QUESTIONS.

3. PRETEST THE QUESTIONS.

4. SELECT THE SAMPLE.

5. INTERVIEW THE SAMPLE.

6. TABULATE AND ANALYZE THE RESULTS.

Now do Assignment #24 on page 94

Organizing Your Facts

When you get into the process of gathering facts, it is important to have a system. You will need to retain all the data which you gather, but it is just as important that once you have the data you keep track of how it fits into what it is you are trying to discover.

In other words, your facts must be assembled so that they fit together. There should be some way of collecting facts so that they can be useful.

You should go about gathering your material using a regular method or procedure. There should be a system in the way you mark or record what it is you are gathering.

It is most disturbing for any researcher to have gone through the trouble of gathering information, particularly when it is gathered first-hand, and then to lose track of the identifying aspects of material that can be obtained once and once only. This can be especially disconcerting. Doing the work once should be enough. We would not want to double work needlessly.

There are some basic means and methods which one can use in order to gather information. Note cards, notebooks, or electronic recording devices are some basic means by which one can record information.

Regardless of which means one prefers, there are basic methods that should be included in the way one records information on each card, each notebook sheet, or cassette tape.

3 WHW

The "3 WHW" is an abbreviated way of identifying the reportorial questions: *Who? When? Where? How? Why?* Keeping your eye on these questions can assure you of getting accurate information, properly identified.

Who?

When researching information, whether from the library or the field, it is important to identify *whom* it is you are researching or *who* is your source of information. Be sure to get the first and last names of the individual in question. And in the case of a commonly-heard name— John Smith or John Doe—be sure to get a middle initial as well. Any return trip you may have to make to a text, library, or individual may cause you embarrassment, or worse still, a waste of time.

When?

While no one wants to be overburdened with dates, it is imperative in the case of library resource material that you record the date of publication, and, in the case of survey questions, that you specify the date on which you received your information. With the dates properly recorded, you will be able to define the timelines of your information.

Where?

It is important to identify the relevant locations connected with your research. In the case of field research, knowing where the company or individual resides may be of definite significance. Geography may have a bearing on the usefulness of the information and should be included in case you need it.

How?

How you gathered your information is a question you should be able to answer. In the instance of field research the means by which you got your responses may have importance. That you worked by telephone, mail, or in person is something you should note. Or again, is your data from a secondary source? Is it library research? How you acquired your information should be specified in your report.

Why?

It is significant to know the purpose for which you gathered your information: It will assist you in finalizing the statement of the problem, and it will facilitate the completion of the report for which you have done the research.

Now do Assignment #25 on page 97

ASSIGNMENT #23

Instructions: The situations described below are jumbled—they ramble on and are not clearly stated.

Your job is to rewrite the situations by defining the problem in a clear and simple sentence on the lines provided.

For example, look at the situation below as described by a supervisor in a conversation.

Situation: "There are an awful lot of meetings around this company, and hardly anyone knows who is having a meeting, when, and wherever. There is so many meetings going on you can hardly tell who is suppose to be where. We have a lot of difficulty knowing whether we are suppose to be at one meeting or the other, and who is doing what and where we are losing an awful lot of time and we need something to be done about this because we are cutting into too much time."

Statement of the Problem: *There is no coordination of the meetings held within the company.*

Now work on the situations below, by reducing the situation to a *statement of the problem.*

---

1. Situation:

"It is hard to tell how you can get promoted in this company. You hear something one place and something in another. You get a lot of information by way of the grapevine, and when you ask someone, he tells you one thing— the Personnel Department seems to be telling you something else, and a person who you work with seems to be telling you something else."

Statement of the Problem:

---

2. Situation:

"A guy called up from the United Fund appeal and asked the president of our company, Mr. Warren, for a report on how well our company is supporting United Fund. Some people already give to United Fund by payroll deductions. Some women say that their husbands are already contributing to the United Fund where they work. While others give in their own community. It is difficult to tell how our company is represented with regard to contributions and participation in the United Fund."

Statement of the Problem:

---

3. Situation:

"We had a training course here put on by the American Management Association last month. Some people seemed to like the program, while others didn't seem to get as much out of it. And we were thinking of having the next training program in the series starting next month. Probably we should have some kind of report on this whole thing."

Statement of the Problem:

_____

_____

4. Situation:

"We have had a number of people leave this company within the last year. All of these people were interviewed by the personnel manager. Although he is a little tied up at the moment, we need some kind of report because we are not sure why some of these people are leaving and we would kind of like to get an idea as to whether or not we could do something about it and probably we could if we had some sort of clear picture of why these people are leaving."

Statement of the Problem:

_____

_____

5. Situation:

"I don't know what the story is around here. Some of the secretaries seem to be over their heads in work. Other secretaries seem to have nothing but time on their hands to polish their nails or whatever. Could be that we just don't need all this many secretaries, and perhaps we could retrain and get some of these girls working in other areas where they are needed more. But—it is a little hard to tell, so it would seem that we should investigate the whole thing."

Statement of the Problem:

_____

_____

ASSIGNMENT #24

Instructions: To discover the challenge and difficulties accompanying field research, the student is asked here to take a simple survey.

Use the form which follows to prepare your work. Then survey a number of people as to their preference on some product, service, or idea—such as: a magazine, an insurance program, or a community action proposal—or some item of another category of interest to you.

- State your objectives: what you are trying to find out.
- Specify the product, service, or idea you are evaluating.
- Develop simple survey questions which can be answered by a *yes, no, undecided,* or *don't know* pattern of response.
- Pretest your questions and evaluate them.
- Select a sample audience.
- Interview them with the questions you have prepared.
- Tabulate your results and write a report on your findings on the form that follows.

SURVEY FORM #1

Date _____

First Name — Last Name

Objective: _____

_____

Product, Service, or Idea being evaluated: _____

_____

QUESTIONS

1. _____

_____

_____

Yes ____%   No ____%   Undecided ____%   Don't Know ____%

2. _____

_____

_____

Yes ____%   No ____%   Undecided ____%   Don't Know ____%

3. _____

_____

_____

Yes ____%   No ____%   Undecided ____%   Don't Know ____%

4. _____

_____

_____

Yes ____%   No ____%   Undecided ____%   Don't Know ____%

5. _____

_____

_____

Yes ____%   No ____%   Undecided ____%   Don't Know ____%

SURVEY FORM #2

_____

Date

_____

First Name   —   Last Name

Tabulation and Analysis of Results

_____

_____

_____

_____

_____

_____

_____

_____

_____

_____

_____

_____

_____

_____

_____

_____

_____

_____

_____

ASSIGNMENT #25

Instructions: This assignment is designed to give the student an opportunity to follow through on the ideas regarding sources of information and organization of facts which have been discussed on the preceding pages.

The student should research information from a secondary source—regarding a topic such as one of the following: photocopy service, car rental, calculator, cassette recorder, or some other business related item of equipment.

Assume that your supervisor has described a situation to you. The problem is that the company intends to rent or buy a new photocopy service, car rental, cassette recorder, or another item. It is your job to research information so that the company will have a better idea as to current trends in the use of the item.

To facilitate the gathering of information and to give the student practice in following the guidelines to proper research outlined above, use the form below.

_____

RESEARCH WORKSHEET

_____
Date

_____
Name of Researcher

Statement of Problem: _____

_____

_____

Topic to be researched: _____

Who? _____

_____

_____

When? _____

_____

_____

Where? _____

_____

_____

How? _____

_____

_____

Why? _____

_____

_____

Other: _____

_____

_____

SUMMARY REPORT OF FINDINGS

_____
Date

_____
Name of Researcher

_____

_____

_____

_____

_____

_____

_____

_____

_____

_____

_____

_____

_____

_____

_____

_____

_____

_____

_____

CHAPTER 8
LOGIC IN BUSINESS

In the preceding chapter it was pointed out that the ways of the scientist have become to a great extent the ways of the businessman. This is due to the degree to which businessmen have come to work with the scientist and scientific methods. Even in those sectors of the business world where a scientist may not be part of the personnel of the company, the impact of science has been felt, nonetheless.

The scientific presence is felt, in part, because of the use of scientifically-structured instruments. The use of computers especially illustrates the adaptation of exacting scientific approaches to the gathering of information. In short, the whole decision-making process has very much been affected by the methods of science.

The Prevalence of Logic

This brings us to the topic of this chapter: "Logic in Business."

People in business, like people in other sectors of society, are prone to make errors. Neither man nor man-made machines are perfect. Still the attempt to use scientific and logical approaches to business is not to be taken for granted. Moreover, it is clear to any observer of the business field that (aside from financial flukes and the unexpected surprises that are a natural part of any enterprise day by day) especially in the area of report writing, people attempt to make the "right" decision by thinking in terms of logic.

This chapter, then, will concentrate on the principles of logic.

Reports in business are written so that they add up to something. And, as we pointed out in an earlier chapter, reports customarily add up to a recommendation or a conclusion. Just about everywhere today—the United Nations, the United States Congress, the local city council—people are busy trying to prove a point. Proving a point is essentially what one tries to do with logic.

As a matter of fact, some professions devote themselves almost exclusively to developing recommendations and conclusions through the use of logic and argumentation. Lawyers, for example, earn their livelihood by research and logic—whether or not we agree with the lawyers' version of logic, the pursuit of law and logic is a basic part of their training and part of their practice.

The aspiring businessman should familiarize himself with basic logic for all his communication needs, also. This is especially so for *effective report writing*.

A Definition of Logic

Logic is the science which investigates the principles governing correct or reliable inference.

Definition of Inference

Inference is the process of deriving the strict logical consequences of assumed premises. *Inference* is the process of arriving at some conclusion.

A *conclusion* is the *result* or *outcome*. For example, "One conclusion of the staff meeting was that we decided to expand our product line."

Recommendations

As we have said, a business report will frequently make a recommendation. A *recommendation* is that which serves to *urge* or *advise* a course of action.

A recommendation does not come from thin air. You, the writer, either are asked to research a particular area or you have taken the initiative to do so on your own. This recommendation should be arrived at based on your conclusions or the inferences you arrive at through the evidence you have gathered.

The purpose of the above discussion is to demonstrate the logical connection of one kind of thinking with the next.

A brief review will help emphasize what we have been saying in the above paragraphs:

1. LOGIC INVOLVES WORKING TOWARD INFERENCES.

2. INFERENCES ARE CONCLUSIONS.

3. CONCLUSIONS LEAD TO RECOMMENDATIONS.

4. RECOMMENDATIONS ARE THE HEART OF MANY BUSINESS REPORTS.

To continue now, we repeat: *Recommendations are or should be based on evidence.*

Evidence

Evidence consists of *facts* or *opinions*.

Facts and *opinions* are what you uncover in your research.

A *fact* should be verified or attested to through some reliable source. Ordinarily, facts are presented as something observed in nature. Facts can be established by testimony. Testimony is given by a witness.

Here are four questions by which one can check the reliability of testimony:

1. WAS THERE ACTUALLY AN OPPORTUNITY FOR THE SOURCE OF THE TESTIMONY TO OBSERVE THE EVIDENCE FIRSTHAND?

2. WAS THE INDIVIDUAL OR WITNESS OFFERING TESTIMONY PHYSICALLY ABLE?

3. IS THE WITNESS INTELLECTUALLY CAPABLE OF REPORTING ACCURATELY?

4. IS THE WITNESS TRUSTWORTHY?

Opinion is offered as evidence when facts are not available. Opinion is a belief or judgment that rests on grounds insufficient to produce certainty. If we want to get a good opinion, we try to get an opinion from an authority. In dealing with authorities, we attempt to get the best authority available.

It should be noted that books, doctors, professors, and other so-called authoritative sources are not necessarily authorities. An authority should be, if at all possible, one that the audience (in this case, a business audience) will know and respect.

The authority used for evidence in preparing business reports should be the best, most reliable, and most relevant source of evidence under the circumstances.

How exacting one will be in getting an authority will depend on many factors. Cost will have some bearing as to how much time will be spent in locating an authority. Time is money in business, and the decision as to how extensive to make the search for sources of evidence should be given some consideration.

However, time and money aside for the moment, one can still develop a critical eye and ear in discerning whether or not a magazine, book, or individual is a good up-to-date source of evidence.

Whether dealing with people or print, practice in determining the quality of evidence is important.

Similarly, it is important to develop one's ability to distinguish fact from opinion. Both have the potential to be valuable. Nevertheless, fact is not opinion; and opinion is not fact.

Now do Assignment #26 on page 108

Reasoning

Reasoning is the act or process of moving from evidence to conclusions. For example, we may observe that in a courtroom a jury arrived at the proper decision by valid reasoning; and, consequently, we concur with its decision that a defendant is innocent.

How the jury arrived at its decision is a matter of different possibilities. Reasoning can be of different kinds. We will talk about three basic kinds of reasoning in this chapter: *induction, analogy,* and *deduction.*

Induction

Induction is a kind of reasoning in which one moves from a number of particulars or instances to a generalization. All science is based on the existence of uniformity. The same kind of event in nature always happens in the same way under the same set of conditions.

Human nature is not always as dependable as physical nature. However, it is still possible to reason inductively about human affairs.

After examining a number of instances we take what is known as "The Inductive Leap." This is the process of generalization.

The activity of shopping for a product, for instance, usually leads to the inductive leap. We sample many of certain items—shoes, dresses, suits—on price and style perhaps. We then generalize as to our preference, and, if we have the necessary funds, we make a purchase.

In order to generalize intelligently we have to be careful of two aspects of the evidence we are examining: *quality* and *validity*.

To be reasonably certain that we are generalizing to the best of our ability under the circumstances, we should ask ourselves the following questions:

1. HAVE A FAIR NUMBER OF INSTANCES BEEN USED?

2. ARE THE INSTANCES TYPICAL?

3. CAN THE NEGATIVE INSTANCES BE EXPLAINED?

In short, the best advice for good inductive reasoning comes from the old adage: "Look before you leap." In other words, make sure that you look at enough instances before you generalize.

Analogy

Analogy is a kind of reasoning in which two things or units are compared. In many explanations regarding the heart transplant, the workings of the heart are explained by analogy—a comparison—between the heart and a pump.

Analogy is a useful way of both persuading and explaining—"selling ideas" and "teaching."

Although analogy is useful in communicating for the purpose of persuading and explaining, it should be mentioned that an analogy is not a conclusive process of reasoning. Mistakes can be made by assuming too quickly that two persons, places, things, or ideas are identical simply because they are similar. This is not always the case. Mistakes can readily be made as, indeed, they have been. Nations have gone to war by assuming that two international situations have been the same.

This does not mean that an analogy cannot be effective. It can be a very powerful and useful means of bringing logic and a sound system of comparison into a report.

Deduction

Deduction has to do with reasoning from premises. In deduction the conclusion will be valid if the premises are valid. Deduction works in the reverse of induction. Whereas, you recall, in induction we reason from a series of particulars to a generalization, in deduction, the process is the other way around. That is, in deduction we reason from a general principle to a particular.

In deduction we assume that whatever is true of all instances or members of a class must be true of one instance. If you know that all ducks swim, and that someone who owns a pond has purchased some ducks, you can deduce that these ducks will probably swim in the pond.

In logic, the pattern of such a line of reasoning is called a *syllogism*. The syllogism consists of a generalization—called a *major premise*; a particular statement—called a *minor premise*; and an *inference* drawn from the two—called a *conclusion*.

Expressed as a *syllogism*, what we said would look like the following:

> All ducks swim. (MAJOR PREMISE)
>
> John has a duck. (MINOR PREMISE)
>
> Therefore, John's duck can swim. (CONCLUSION)

It is apparent that no one in everyday conversation will express himself in a formal *syllogism*. In any case, consciously or unconsciously, our minds often go through the *syllogistic* pattern.

For example, with a little knowledge or experience on the topic, you conclude that beer has alcoholic content. Given a can of beer, though you may never have heard of the brand, in a split second, you will reason *deductively*. Perhaps not in formal terms, but the essence of this line of reasoning will cross your mind.

> (All) Beer is one of those beverages that contain alcohol. (MAJOR PREMISE)
>
> This can of liquid is beer. (MINOR PREMISE)
>
> Therefore, this can of liquid is one of those beverages that contain alcohol. (CONCLUSION)

Deduction is a kind of reasoning that is used to prove things, whereas *induction* is generally used to discover things.

This brief introduction to lines of reasoning is not to be considered complete by any stretch of the imagination. There is the "if—then" and "either—or" line of reasoning that is not considered here. There are other patterns of reasoning that could be explained and amplified. The human mind is a complex mechanism and can reason in more ways than can be delineated in these few pages—probably in more ways than man himself can understand. However, for the newcomer to serious discussion and logical research, the framework provided in this chapter will provide a structure of terms and ideas which can prove very useful.

Fallacies

Fallacies are errors in reasoning. Sports fans know all too well that errors are very much a part of the game.

A hit on errors, for example, brings to mind much that could be said about the ways in which errors are committed. Recognizing errors and knowing what to do about them is very much a part of playing and appreciating many games in the world of sports.

So, too, in business one must guard against errors. Not only in simple calculations but also in working with ideas, one must be careful not to make errors himself, or have fallacious reasoning passed off to him as valid and true reasoning.

In this chapter we will consider four kinds of fallacies: *equivocation, begging the question, non sequitur,* and *ignoring the question.*

Equivocation

Equivocation means the use of ambiguous expressions, especially in order to mislead or hedge; it also means using terms that have two or more meanings.

Here is an example:

"Colleges usually have student unions; industries have labor unions."

The word "union" is used *equivocally*. A student union is a place for relaxation, refreshments, and friendly reception. A labor union is a structure for bargaining for better wages, working conditions, and employee benefits.

Begging the Question

Begging the question means the poisoning of propositions with "loaded" terms such as *bad, unsanitary,* and so on.

Here is an example:

"The immoral and harmful practice of premarital sex is a question of grave concern in our society today."

In the above statement the question is whether or not premarital sex is good or evil in our society, but the argument has been poisoned by the use of the words *immoral* and *harmful*—which portray premarital sex negatively before the argument begins.

The fallacy of *begging the question* sometimes takes the form called "reasoning in a circle."

For instance, observe the following:

"If we develop the resources of the country, people will have a higher standard of living. If they have a higher standard of living, they will become more ambitious and will fully develop the resources of the country."

Non Sequitur

Non sequitur is a Latin expression meaning an inference or a conclusion which does not follow from the premises. Literally it means "it does not follow."

Here is an illustration:

"A man sees a black cat cross the road. Soon afterwards he is involved in an automobile accident. He infers that, since the accident came after his encounter with the black cat, therefore the cat caused the accident." (SUPER-STITIONS AND POPULAR BELIEFS LEAD, OF COURSE, TO A GREAT MANY SUCH FALLACIES.)

Ignoring the Question

Ignoring the question means shifting to irrelevancies: The question is ignored when the ground of the argument is shifted in some way from the real issues to false issues.

Here is an illustration:

"During the recent campaign for nominations for the Presidency of the United States, William Collier was asked by newscasters about his qualifications for the Presidency. His reply was 'Let me say this: When the American people go to the polls they will express their feelings about a need for a change in leadership.'"

Now do Assignment #27 on page 109

ASSIGNMENT #26

Instructions: After the statements below, on the blanks to the right, write down the word *fact* or *opinion*.

Make a judgment as to whether or not the statement signifies something that is essentially a fact or fundamentally an opinion.

———————————

1. He may very well be afraid to take on such responsibility. _____

2. American astronauts have been on the moon. _____

3. Civil Rights legislation has been passed in the United States in the last ten years. _____

4. Some scientists predict that we could be eating all synthetic or artificial foods by the year 2000. _____

5. The American dollar has undergone a devaluation on the world market. _____

6. The Supreme Court is the highest court in the United States. _____

7. There is a reasonable chance that we will see a woman president in the White House within the next few years. _____

8. The best way to deal with inflation may be to allow it to work itself out by supply and demand in the market place with a minimum of governmental regulations. _____

9. The Administration will very likely provide us with a good government. _____

10. Mount Everest, a mountain in the Himalayas, is the highest mountain in the world; it measures 29,028 feet. _____

ASSIGMENT #27

Instructions: Select the fallacy name which best identifies the kind of error in reasoning made in the examples below. Enter the appropriate fallacy on the space after each number—**equivocation, begging the question, non sequitur,** or **ignoring the question.**

Some of the fallacious statements below can be considered more than one kind of error. Select one, but be prepared to discuss the possibilities.

_____

1. Parking areas and city police are both dense on the Brown College Campus.

2. The number of women who become great business leaders is small; therefore, women are not as intelligent as men.

3. A local school official was asked if the people living in a nearby ghetto were receiving a better education. His reply: "Our community has spent an additional two million dollars on education."

4. Art Weidel, a man of integrity, who understands and can solve the problems of our city, should be elected as our next mayor.

5. *Look* is bigger than *Life*.

6. A man and his wife were arguing about a telephone bill and the only thing his wife said was—"You don't love me."

7. A man decides to miss Mass on Sunday in order to go fishing. While fishing Sunday morning, he slips into the deep water, losing most of his fishing equipment. He infers that since he did not attend Mass, therefore, his missing Mass caused the accident—he was punished by the Good Lord.

8. X Company went on strike. After the settlement, the company prospered. Therefore, strikes are necessary for a company to prosper.

9. The unhealthy practice of dissent has damaged the appearance of the United States.

10. The police arrested the young couple for parking in the parking lot.

CHAPTER 9
SHORT REPORT FORMS

So far, we have covered means for providing avenues by which the writer can improve his ability to write and his ability to think. All of the material in your text has been leading up to the writing of reports. You have already had some sample experiences in business report writing. Chapter Three gave you some initial opportunities in report writing. In this chapter we will concentrate on short report forms and how to work with them.

Short reports are often looked on as the real "work horses" of business communication.

Though the short report has some similarities to the long report, there are, nonetheless, differences. The short report tends to be less formal, shorter in length—obviously—and is frequently written on an established form or in a routine format.

The kinds of short reports that will be treated in this chapter are called the *letter report*, the *form report*, and the *short informal report*.

The Letter Report

It should be clear by now that there is more than one way to report. A report is simply a matter of communicating information, suggestions, or recommendations. And, of course, in this text we are limiting ourselves to *written report* writing.

There are certain reasons why the familiar business letter is a good form for the purpose of report writing. The layout of the business letter is one that is generally familiar to most people. It does not require special indoctrination for most of us to learn how to use it.

The letter is a flexible medium of communication. On one hand, it allows for ceremonious, official, and formal styles of writing. On the other hand, the letter can also be unceremonious, natural, and informal. The letter has the capacity to be a more direct means of communication—written *by* someone *for* someone. In connection with this last point, it should be said that the letter as a means of reporting should not be overused. There are other alternatives that should be considered before overusing the letter as a short report.

Directness is the essential requisite of a good short report. In general format, the letter report will resemble any good business letter—with perhaps minor variations, depending on the length of the letter. Some modifications which are used, for example, are subheadings underscored and/or sideheadings that are included to highlight the sections of a fairly lengthy letter.

The following are some requisites of a letter report:

Authorization: Indicate the individual who authorized the writing of the report and the date on which he authorized it.

Objective: Indicate the objective—the aim or intent of your letter report.

Scope: Indicate for the reader the extent of the subject matter to be reported on. Tell the reader the span of information on which you are reporting.

Conclusion: The letter report should contain conclusions. It should indicate what you have inferred from your investigation, and the recommendations which follow from your conclusions.

Now do Assignment #28 on page 116

AUTO TREND, INC.
525 Market Street
Newark, N. J. 02969

February 2, 19--

Parts Unlimited
250 North Main Street
Providence, Rhode Island 02906

Dear Mr. Doorlan:

On January 2 Mr. Albert Stone, Vice President of Sales, authorized a study for your company. The purpose of the study was to determine the market potential in the New England region for replacement parts on imported automobile stereo and other sound equipment.

A comprehensive report will be forwarded to you by the end of this month. However, we can at this time indicate to you the pertinent findings of the study.

Our research staff recommends that you take steps to keep higher quality imported automobile stereo sound parts and components in your warehouse stock. Our survey indicates that consumer interest in higher quality merchandise is sufficient to warrant investment in this area. Less expensive parts and equipment are: 1) interchangeable with domestic brands (currently in abundance); or 2) discarded (or traded) by the consumer.

With respect to your recent auto parts company's acquisitions, we recommend that you sell off the inexpensive stock; and that you hold the better lines for your spring promotional. We are in the process of preparing a definitive analysis of key market centers and will include this with the other data of the study in the complete report.

Very truly yours,

H. R. Dunning
Director Market Research

Figure 1.   Letter Report

112

A great amount of written reporting in industry and business is accomplished by means of report forms. Generally less elegant in form and content, they perform an important communication function all the same.

There is a wide variety of routine forms for reports. A sampling of report forms will include the following: absentee report, daily report of goods received, daily report of shipments, expense reports, reports of goods received, report of goods returned, salesmen's call reports, and shipping department's daily reports.

The specimen which follows is an illustration of the "Salesmen's Daily Call Report."

SALESMAN'S CALL REPORT

☐ Prospect ☐ Customer Date _____

Firm _____

Address _____ City _____

Party seen _____

Comment _____

_____

_____

_____

_____

_____

_____

_____

_____

_____

_____

_____

_____

_____

_____

_____

_____

SEND REPORTS TO OFFICE EACH DAY

Salesman _____

Figure 1a. Salesman's Call Report

Routine report forms specify the kind of information that is required. For example, a receiving report form will have printed on it such needed information as the following: purchase order number, department name, received from, shipped from, delivered by, charges, quantity of materials, description of materials, and weight. There may be other blanks or boxes for a description of the merchandise involved.

It is possible in filling out forms to learn from practice. However, since forms are so diversified, experience on the job is probably the best way to learn how to fill out routine report forms.

The Short Informal Report

Having discussed the letter report and the routine report form, we will now study the short informal report.

Superficially, the letter report appears to be like other business letters. The difference between the business letter and the formal business report lies in what the report does and says.

The short informal report resembles the long formal report in appearance, more than the letter report or the routine report form. But the short informal report communicates on a much more limited basis.

The short informal report may communicate information, suggestions, and recommendations. It may supply a description of a production process, a progress report, or, in one way or another, supply some useful or meaningful message.

Sometimes a distinction is made between reports that are informational and those that are interpretive. Informational reports convey knowledge to the reader—knowledge of facts which the reader, presumably, needs in order either to make decisions or for other purposes. Interpretive reports go beyond communicating data or information. They furnish what is implied in the word *interpret*—interpretation. Interpretive reports provide an explanation; they attempt to explain, to enlighten, or to render some meaning or significance of the implications found in the data of the report.

What, then, is the structure of the short informal report? It is fundamentally the same as the long report, except that it is much more limited in scope. The following outline is appropriate to the composition of the short informal report.

1. SUMMARY OF THE REPORT

2. INTRODUCTION TO THE REPORT

3. DATA AND EXPLANATION

4. CONCLUSIONS AND RECOMMENDATIONS

5. APPENDIX

Explanation and Clarification of Parts of the Report

Summary of the Report

In the summary of the short informal report, the conclusions and recommendations are briefly stated. There is no building up to or creating of curiosity. *Short and to the point*, the sum and substance of the report are stated.

Introduction to the Report

The objectives and limitations of the report are laid out in this section.

Data and Explanation

The facts or information of the report are analyzed in this next section. Prior experience of the company with the problem area is described. Related research may be touched upon. Summarized in brief are the research, experiences, and work involved of the personnel, scientists, engineers, or others who have dealt with the topic of the report—or comparable problems are noted and discussed.

Conclusions and Recommendations

In this section of the report, an attempt is made to add up the research, study, or investigation. The consequences of various courses of action may be spelled out, and a general plan or course of action is recommended.

Appendix

The appendix is used to provide visual aids—graphs, charts, pictures, or tables—that will help the reader of the report to understand better what the report is about. Ordinarily an appendix is construed to be supplementary. It is understood that the reader will consult the appendix if he has difficulty reading or understanding the report. Or in the event that the reader wishes to gather a more detailed explanation of the report, he will consult the appendix. Data which is part of the background of the report may also be inserted in the appendix. But since the appendix is supplementary reading, the writer may insert materials in the appendix without worrying that he is necessarily tying up the reader. Very often the materials put in the appendix are more than what is required for the actual comprehension of the report, but may merely be included in the appendix to demonstrate the completeness of the work done in preparing the report, or included as background to be used in exploring the matter further.

Now do Assignment #29 on page 116

115

ASSIGNMENT #28

Instructions: Assume that someone requested a report from you. That someone may be your instructor, the dean of your school, the president of the student senate at your school, your employer (if you work part-time or full-time) — or someone else.

Assume that this party has asked for a report on a recent trip, extracurricular activity at your school, facilities at your school (library or other), study conditions, work conditions — or some other subject of interest to you.

Respond to this request for a report by writing a *letter report*. Remember the requisites of a good letter report:

1. *Authorization*
2. *Objective*
3. *Scope*
4. *Conclusion*

Use Fig. 1, page 113, as a model. For the completion of this assignment, use personal, business, or college stationery—whichever is appropriate for the letter report you write.

ASSIGNMENT #29

Instructions: This assignment is given in order to help the student gain a better appreciation of the kind of research, thinking, and writing that goes into a short informal report. The form provided on the next work pages will allow the student to do a short informal research report.

Assume that you work for a particular company and that your supervisor has asked you for a report on a topic of interest to you both. The topic (for the purposes of this report) may be some sort of business enterprise.

Begin this project by checking a business-oriented newspaper such as the *Wall Street Journal* or the classified section of *The New York Times*. Look under "Business Connections" or "Business Opportunities" or a similar kind of heading. Locate a business opportunity, such as an investment fund, a franchise, a business system, or a business connection that you might want to invest in, if you had the time and money.

Then research this business enterprise—company, fund, or franchise—in the library. (Review Chapter Four on *Library Resources.*) Prepare a report using the form on page 117. You will probably want to prepare your material roughly first and then enter it on the form.

Note: For the appendix it will be a good idea to Xerox or photocopy materials out of magazines, newspapers, or books for the purpose of supplying the report with appropriate graphs, charts, tables, or other diagrams that are needed to amplify and clarify the topic of your report.

If the form provided is too short in space, use the format as a model for an independently-prepared report.

SHORT COMPANY REPORT FORM

FROM: _____   DATE: _____

TO: _____

SUBJECT: _____

SUMMARY

_____
_____
_____
_____
_____
_____
_____
_____
_____
_____

INTRODUCTION: _____
_____
_____
_____
_____
_____
_____
_____
_____

ANALYSIS OF DATA: _____

_____

_____

_____

_____

_____

_____

_____

_____

CONCLUSIONS AND RECOMMENDATIONS: _____

_____

_____

_____

_____

_____

_____

_____

_____

APPENDIX: (see attached enclosures)

CHAPTER 10

THE MEMORANDUM

In the last chapter, we talked about various forms of the short report—the *letter report,* the *routine report form,* and the *short informal report.* In this chapter we will talk about the *memorandum.*

We defined *memorandum* earlier in the text. We defined it, in general, as something written to be remembered—*an informal reminder or record of some act or event.* More elaborately defined, a memorandum is an instrument or statement intended to provide a record of a transaction—rather than that which serves as a basis for action in itself.

The memorandum is characterized by informality and often in business it is a kind of basic medium used to send notes from one individual to another—sent on an interoffice or intercompany basis.

The memorandum can range from a simple scribbling on a sheet of paper to something quite formalized. On the average, in business and industry, the memorandum follows some sort of predetermined form. One would find in the introductory portion the date, who originated the memorandum, to whom it is addressed, and the subject matter will follow below.

How similar is a memorandum to a formal report? The memorandum can be something distinct and apart from the formal report, both in its brevity and its informality. On the other hand, there are grey areas of communication where a memorandum is hardly distinguishable from a short report. In this chapter, we will discuss the problems of writing memorandums.

The memorandum tends to be a less important medium of communication. However, all that depends on what is in the message. A simple suggestion can be sent on a method for the improvement of a company operation, and it may be scribbled as a quickly dashed-off memorandum. A brief, handwritten memorandum can accompany a special report that needs to be routed throughout a company. A brief memorandum can serve as an explanatory note or serve as an "ice breaker" of other sorts as well.

Then, too, the memorandum can be something more urgent. For example, in a crisis situation, a memorandum may be the best means of calling certain people together for an emergency meeting. When face-to-face, oral communication or the telephone will not do the job, the memorandum often comes forward as a trusty means of communication.

Abuse of the Memorandum

With the advent of photocopying machines, the memorandum has been "used to death" in many companies. The ease with which managers can reproduce multiple copies of a memorandum via the facilities of a photocopier or Xerox machine has made the memorandum an abused means of communication.

The mistaken assumption has arisen that if two memorandums can be sent out to good effect, four can be doubly effective. And if one hundred memorandums can do a creditable job, four hundred memorandums can do four times as good a job. Of course, this kind of reasoning is fallacious, especially when those who are not informed, interested, or involved in the transactions addressed in the message are simply sent the memo gratuitously.

The fact that the memorandum has been abused as a means of communication does not say that it is not an important communications channel. When it is used properly and with discretion, the memorandum remains an important communication alternative.

The Carbonized Memorandum

With increased sophistication in printing processes and the growing number of modern business form companies, memorandums of all sorts, sizes, and shapes have come into being.

As an illustration, there are *carbonized* memorandums. With the carbonized memorandums the manager can write or type his message on the first page—ordinarily a white sheet. A separate space on the side of the memorandum or beneath is so arranged so that the party receiving the memorandum can reply directly on the *same sheet*. Carbon sheets are already in place so that the sender can automatically get two copies, sending one and keeping one. There are those carbonized memorandums that are laid out so that the sender can snap out a middle yellow sheet (or other colored copy) for his follow-up reply. The sender can mail the white and pink copies, allowing the receiver to hold on to a third copy and return his (the receiver's) stated message on the original. The recipient merely writes or typewrites his response on the carbonized copy, keeps a pink copy for his files, and mails the white copy back to the originator.

Figure 2 below is a specimen of the format of the popular *carbonized* memorandum.

DR. BURTON L. FISCHMAN

Smithfield College, No. Bryant, Massachusetts 09416 (617) 421-2980, Ext. 973

MESSAGE	REPLY
TO _____	DATE _____
_____	_____
_____	_____
DATE _____	
BY _____	Signed _____

Figure 2. Carbonized Memo Form

Variations of the Memorandum

There are many variations on the principle of the carbonized memorandum. They are used with a great deal of success in business. What many executives like about the carbonized memorandum is that it is used exclusively for the communication in question; it is not likely to be abused as has the nicely type-written memorandum which is copied a countless number of times by the Xerox machine.

The carbonized memorandum is a useful means of communication when the sender wants a quick response, or when he wants to be clear about what is both sent and received. In short, it accomplishes efficient and inexpensive two-way, written communication.

There are many business form companies that print all sorts of forms. These forms allow you to get your message across in traditional or contemporary styling. There are personalized memorandums with name imprints of the individual. There are those which will have the company logos, or company trademark, company address, and other details.

There are memorandums which are combination letter and report forms. There are memorandums which have humorous symbols, pictures, or jokes on them that are sometimes used for a change of pace.

There are *transmittal* memorandums with checklists of instructions for the receiver. Such memorandums can be done up in attractive, personalized forms and in compact size. These are ideal for routine check-off communications with conveniences for standard repeating messages. The reader is invited to study Figure 3 below, a *transmittal* memorandum.

TRANSMITTAL MEMO
from
Burton L. Fischman

TO: _____   DATE: _____

☐ For your information   ☐ Please reply and return copy to me

☐ Your comments, please   ☐ Review and reply to

☐ Review and call me   _____

☐ Review and forward to

☐ Review and file

                                   ☐ Attach previous correspondence
☐ Review and return to me   and return to me

COMMENTS/REPLY

_____

_____

_____

Figure 3. Transmittal Memo

The Tone of a Memorandum

Two characteristics of the memorandum are: 1) it is likely to be for a short-lived purpose or duration, and 2) it is likely to be informal. The style of writing in the memorandum is likely to be an informal style, and incomplete sentences are expected. But whether the memorandum is formal or not, *tone* is important.

Tone refers to quality, pitch, and strength of voice. Although tone usually refers to sounds which we hear, tone can refer to words in a written communication as well.

When reading a memorandum to oneself, a tone of voice comes across. In other words, there is a mood or attitude which is expressed in written communication. And the writer of a memorandum should keep in mind that his own attitude toward the subject communicated about and his relationship to his reading audience is important.

One of the difficulties in writing in the proper tone for a business situation is that the individual sending out a memorandum (supervisor, manager, or someone else) may justifiably be angry about what one or two workers have done. Nevertheless, if the memorandum is sent to more than just the one or two parties who have been negligent or clearly in need of reprimand, the tone of the message must be modulated.

One should be careful, then, to keep in mind the total audience receiving a memorandum, so that the tone is appropriate for the audience addressed. It is better to take a positive mental attitude when a memorandum is going to many people.

For an illustration of a positively worded and phrased memorandum, the specimen on the next page is included. It has been written in response to a situation in which there has been abuse of company Xerox facilities.

Notice that the memorandum is tactful and diplomatic. Presumably if the situation does not improve, the individuals who aggravate the situation can then be dealt with on a one-to-one basis. There may be no need for a blanket accusation. Blanket accusations may have a negative effect on the morale of an otherwise productive department.

Now do Assignment #30 on page 126

The Progress Report

A progress report is a periodic communication on one's growth, improvement, development, or advancement on an assignment or project. The progress report may be one of a kind, delivered in answer to a request by your supervisor. The progress report may also be a routine communication that a company requires weekly, monthly, or at some other specified time interval.

TO: All Personnel

FROM: Robert L. Smith, Manager

SUBJECT: Use of the Office Xerox Copying Machine

Your cooperation would be appreciated in observing the following guidelines on use of the Xerox Copying Machine:

The Xerox should not be used for items of a personal nature.

The only materials that should be duplicated are those documents which absolutely require a second copy.

Observance of the above procedures, I am sure, will result in improved service to all departments, as well as a substantial saving to your company.

Figure 4. Sample of Inter-office Memo

Since, as the name implies, you are communicating on the nature of your advancement in an assignment or project, a progress report is going to be primarily informational. It is not likely to contain ideas, recommendations, suggestions, or analyses.

In a fair-sized company, a progress report may be part of routine information gathering which each supervisor is asked to tend to as part of his job. Progress reports, in such an operation, are sent up the ladder to keep top managers informed—so that decisions can be made on *current* information.

The content of a progress report should include: 1) times; 2) dates; 3) how the assignment or project is doing in relation to planning; and 4) problems or difficulties encountered along the line. There may also be a projection as to the anticipated completion dates for part or all of the work.

Since it is safe to assume that the supervisor or whoever is going to read the progress report is informed on the nature of the project, the progress report serves as a means of *updating* the reader—giving him an overview about the past, present, and future. The reader is going to be on the lookout for anything unanticipated that might have cropped up, and anything that will necessitate a change of plans.

It is a good idea for the student or the businessman to keep a file of the progress reports he sends out. It may be advisable to follow the same format if it turns out to be serviceable. And the information on the memorandum may be useful for future reference.

See Figure 5, page 125, a specimen progress report.

Now do Assignment #31 on page 128

AMERICAN INTERNATIONAL INSURANCE

FROM: John R. Newman, Director   **DATE:**   November 1, 19--
                  Hospital Utilization

TO: Jerry Herman
                Executive Vice President

SUBJECT: Progress on the Alpha Hospital Plan

Research Progress—September 15 to November 1

On September 15 a questionnaire was mailed to the directors of one hundred hospitals in New England that are currently covered by the Alpha Hospital Plan. By November 1 sixty-eight directors responded with completed questionnaires.

Jack D'Amiano is presently computing the results. Within the next few days he will forward his report to my Research Department for analysis.

Plans for the Future

On December 1 it is expected that any late questionnaires will be in and that a final tabulation can be made. Our final analysis should be completed by the Executive Staff meeting scheduled for December 17.

On or by December 13 a copy of the report will be sent to all staff members, so that all interested personnel will have an opportunity to review our findings and my recommendations prior to the meeting.

Figure 5. Progress Report

ASSIGNMENT #30

Instructions: Rewrite the memorandum below in your own name with the following assumptions in mind:

1. that you are the supervisor of a fair size department—that is, more than a few;

2. that there has been abuse of stationery supplies both for company and personal use;

3. that this situation has developed, as far as you can tell, during the past month;

4. that you, the supervisor, have not said anything thus far on the matter; and

5. that this will be the first communication on this subject from you.

TO: All Personnel **DATE:**

FROM: Robert L. Smith, Manager

SUBJECT: Improper and wasteful use of stationery supplies

As regards what has been brought to my attention regarding the excessive and unjustified use of the stationery supplies, it has been brought to my attention that company employees have been wasting company supplies. Let's all straighten this situation out immediately.

NOTE: USE THE FORM ON PAGE 127 FOR YOUR REWRITE OF THIS MEMORANDUM.

MEMORANDUM

TO: DATE:

FROM:

SUBJECT:

_____
_____
_____
_____
_____
_____
_____
_____
_____
_____
_____
_____
_____
_____
_____
_____
_____
_____
_____
_____
_____
_____
_____

ASSIGNMENT #31

Instructions: Using the form below, report on a subject of interest to you or your class. Your topic might be progress in a course, a study project, a new job, a committee on which you serve, a building or construction project in the area, or some other subject of interest to you.

Study Figure 5, page 125, and use the form below as a guide to your writing.

PROGRESS REPORT

FROM: **DATE:**

TO:

SUBJECT:

Progress for Time Period   to

_____

_____

_____

_____

_____

_____

_____

_____

_____

_____

_____

Plans for the Future

_____

_____

_____

_____

CHAPTER 11
WRITING THE FORMAL REPORT
PART I

In Chapter 10 we worked on writing a memorandum. In this chapter we will take up the bigger challenge toward which this text works: *writing the formal or long report*. In a sense, all that we have studied in this course so far is the preparation for writing a long report. Because of the many-faceted nature of the long report, the student or businessman is called upon to use his total experiences and mental resources in writing a good one.

The Organization of a Report

Organization is an essential characteristic of the well-written business report. The formal report has various components, each with its particular function to perform. The composition of reports varies tremendously in business. Yet, certain common elements appear repeatedly in the vast majority of formal reports. These elements will be studied in this chapter and the next.

The elements will be defined and explained. Samples will be included to show how these elements add up to a complete formal report.

The Elements of a Formal Report

The elements most commonly found in the formal report are: the cover, the flyleaf, the title page, the letter of transmittal, the table of contents, the summary or abstract, the body of the report, the bibliography, and the appendix.

There are other elements which the writer may want to add, such as: a frontispiece (an illustrated leaf preceding the title page), a copyright statement, a letter of acceptance, a letter of approval, a dedication, a foreword, a preface, a table of illustrations, and an index. However, these parts are not essential. They are added as needed: when the company or supervisor authorizing the report requests it, or when the individual writing the report feels that the report would be improved by the addition of another element.

For purposes of clarity, it may help to see the report divided into three sections: *preliminary parts*, *body of the report*, and *ending parts*. See Figure 6.

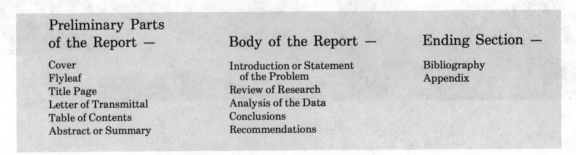

Preliminary Parts of the Report —	Body of the Report —	Ending Section —
Cover	Introduction or Statement of the Problem	Bibliography
Flyleaf		Appendix
Title Page	Review of Research	
Letter of Transmittal	Analysis of the Data	
Table of Contents	Conclusions	
Abstract or Summary	Recommendations	

Figure 6. Elements of the Report

Explanation of Report Elements

Cover

A variety of kinds of covers may be used for the long report. Paper, plastic, or other types of covers may be used. Some businesses or organizations have their own special jackets (with their own logos and design) into which their reports are inserted.

The practice of the company for which you are working will determine the standards and style of the cover you will use for the long report.

The Flyleaf

The flyleaf is a blank sheet of paper which ordinarily goes before the title page. Although it is not entirely necessary, a flyleaf does add a favorable appearance and connotes a degree of formality.

Title Page

The title page is a means of completely naming the report. Titles in the arts are often imaginative and designed to get attention. Such titles may not necessarily define the specific purpose of the work. The title of a report should be specific, precise, and descriptive of the report to follow.

The title page is most helpful to the reader when it communicates the *general* thrust of the report, while at the same time it is *specific* enough to give the reader a sense of the limitations of the report.

For example, this title would be overly brief for a formal report:

"A Personnel Research Study"

This title gives the reader a general indication of the nature of study, but the title does not specify within the area of personnel what is to be studied.

The following title would be much more appropriate:

"A Personnel Study of Effectiveness of Young People
in Executive Positions in the McCormic Corporation"

This title is much more useful to the reader in indicating the general nature of the study as well as providing a definition of its limitations.

There are obviously some questions which this title leaves unanswered. For instance: What is meant by "young"? Which "executive positions"? and so on.

However, these questions can be answered in the report. Nevertheless, the title does give the reader enough preliminary assistance in helping him decide whether or not he will want to read the report. This is the kind of preliminary help the title should give.

Along with the title on the title page should appear: the *name(s)* of the *author(s)*; the *name*, the *address*, and the *complete name* of the *organization* or company for which the report was written; and finally the *date* on which the report was submitted.

There may be other particulars regarding the place, arrangements, funding, or other information which may be needed in order to identify the report properly. A sample of a typical title page appears in Figure 7, page 133.

A PERSONNEL STUDY OF EFFECTIVENESS OF YOUNG PEOPLE

IN EXECUTIVE POSITIONS IN THE McCORMIC CORPORATION

Prepared for

Mr. R. H. McCormic, President
32970 Norwood Boulevard
Boston, Massachusetts

Prepared by

Mr. Winston L. Murphy
Personnel Assistant
American Research Associates
2162 Massachusetts Avenue
Boston, Massachusetts

December 3, 19--

Figure 7. Title Page

The letter of transmittal accompanies and explains the purpose of the business report. It serves as a means of conveying the report to the supervisor or the individual who gave authorization for the writing of the report.

In the order of the report components, the letter of transmittal comes right after the title page and before the table of contents. On occasion the letter of transmittal is sent separately. Ordinarily it is bound in with the report.

The letter of transmittal repeats the instructions given in the original authorization (instructions to proceed with the assignment). The letter also notes that the writer has proceeded with the assignment and that he has, in fact, completed it.

The letter of transmittal may give an overview of the purposes and accomplishments of the report. In so doing, the letter may stress the requisites and aims of the report, noting in brief summary the recommendations and conclusions to be found in the report.

In short, the letter of transmittal locates the report in time and place in the business organization in which it is written.

In style the letter of transmittal tends to be written in a cordial personal manner rather than the objective impersonal manner characteristic of the rest of the report.

See Figure 8, page 135, for a sample letter of transmittal.

ALGROS CORPORATION
555 Commonwealth Avenue
Boston, Massachusetts 02116

March 2, 19--

Mr. Albert Burding
Senior Personnel Manger
Algros Corporation
227 Lane Avenue
New York, NY 10002

Dear Mr. Burding:

I am pleased to forward to you a copy of the enclosed report, "Women Executives in the Algros Corporation." As you will recall, you authorized this project in your letter to me of January 10, 19--.

It is the consensus of those who participated in the investigation contained in the report that the steps taken to place women in top management positions in the last two years have been successful. There has been more cost attached to the development program than was anticipated. However, the results in managerial effectiveness and positive public relations more than compensate for the time and money spent.

As is stated in the report, our conclusion is that it is more effective to develop executive talent within the corporation than to recruit new personnel from without. The recommendation is that our present personnel policies in this area be continued.

This has been a gratifying report to prepare, and I trust it will prove helpful to all concerned. Please feel free to call on me if I can be of any further assistance.

Very truly yours,

Lloyd T. Melroy
Assistant Personnel Manager

Figure 8. Letter of Transmittal

Table of Contents

The table of contents is an overview of the materials in your report. It is synonymous with (or the same as) an outline of the report. It shows the reader the order in which your report sections will appear, and it designates the page on which each part of your report will begin.

The extent of detail of the table of contents should be in relationship to the extent of the report. In other words, a fairly brief report, say of eight to ten pages, may not need a table of contents—the reader may find it superfluous. A report running ten to fifteen pages will probably be made better by a table of contents. A report running thirty to forty pages will need a detailed table of contents as a guide through the report.

Two basic ways of handling the table of contents are:

1. A *simple table of contents* in which only the section headings are included.

2. A *detailed table of contents* in which the subtopic headings are also included.

Ease of reading is the objective, so that a decision to supply a simple or detailed table of contents should be made on the basis of *need*. A detailed table of contents should *not* be furnished strictly for show.

Figure 9, page 137, is a sample of a *simple table of contents*.

TABLE OF CONTENTS

Figure 9. Simple Table of Contents

The summary or abstract is a brief, condensed rendition of the report. It concentrates on giving the reader the essentials of the report.

The reader will find that this part of the report goes by various names: *summary, abstract, synopsis,* and *epitome.*

There are fine distinctions that some writers have in mind with the use of these terms. Nevertheless, the aim of all, insofar as the long formal report is concerned, is the same—and that is to reduce the entire report to a capsule form for the convenience of the reader.

As we have already said, the writer of business reports differs from the fictional writer in that the business writer does not tease the reader into reading the entire work. The summary provided at the beginning of the business report is, in the best sense of the word, *businesslike—brief and to the point.* The reader—supervisor, manager, or whoever—should be able to read your summary and make a decision as to whether he will want to read the complete report.

The challenge in writing a good summary is to come up with a true miniature of the report proper. That is, the summary must reflect in miniature the unity and emphasis of ideas which are found in the entire report.

Refer to Figure 10, page 139, for an example of a summary.

Now do Assignments #32 and #33 on page 140

SUMMARY

There have been varied results from studies of women in executive positions. The preponderance of these reports has not been favorable to the performance and use of women in executive or top management positions.

Prior studies done in our company by Smith and Murphy indicate that, taken individually, women in executive roles have been effective and make noteworthy contributions to the growth of the corporation. But, as a general practice, recruiting women is not a fruitful effort in itself.

The results of this report indicate that the prior investigation of the matter needs updating for two significant reasons: 1) the number of women working for the corporation was too small from which to draw significant generalizations; and 2) generalizations on work performance were oversimplified, lacking analysis in light of current research.

The assessment of performance in the corporation in this investigation has generated several conclusions. Among the more noteworthy are: 1) Women who have worked for the corporation for a number of years and have "come up through the ranks" have been successful (with additional training and/or education) in the jump to top management positions; and 2) Women who have been brought to the company via our own field recruiting or agency service have not performed well.

The recommendation of this report is that if the corporation chooses to pursue a policy of increased use of women in top management, additional funds should be allocated for a management development program for women.

It is also recommended that any recruitment of executive women done outside the company be done on a much more selective basis than in the past.

Figure 10. Sample Summary

ASSIGNMENT #32

(This assignment will be done on separate sheets. Use the space on this page for ideas, notes, or reminders that will be helpful to you in completing this project.)

Instructions: Using Figure 8, page 135, as a model, write a letter of transmittal to Mr. Gifford A. Brown using the following information:

1. Assume that Mr. Brown authorized a study on minority employment practices, inflation, energy problems, or some other subject of interest to you on December 12, 19--.

2. Acknowledge the fact that you received help from your professor and some library staff personnel in completing an investigation on the subject, but state that essentially the report contains your own ideas on the subject.

3. End your report by thanking Mr. Brown for the opportunity to do the research study. Tell him you hope that the report will prove to be helpful, and that if he has any further questions he should communicate with you for the purpose of setting up a conference.

ASSIGNMENT #33

(This assignment will be done on separate sheets. Use the space on this page for ideas, notes, or reminders that will be helpful to you in completing this project.)

Instructions: Following the model of the summary abstract, Figure 10, page 139, write a summary of a report on some business situation or condition that was written for a special time, place, and situation in a company or corporation.

Not all reports include summaries. Select one lacking a summary or whose summary is too brief in your judgment; and write one along the lines of the "summary" in this chapter.

Check the library of your college or school, public library in the area for business resources that might be appropriate for resource material needed for completion of this assignment.

CHAPTER 12
WRITING THE FORMAL REPORT
PART II

In Chapter Eleven we talked about the preliminary or prefatory parts of the long report. We talked about the cover, the flyleaf, the letter of transmittal, the summary, and the table of contents. We discussed the nature of each part of the report, and we had an opportunity to practice our skills in writing a letter of transmittal and a summary abstract.

These items are basic. Elimination of any of these parts would detract from the effectiveness of a long report.

What is the purpose of the preliminary parts of the long report?—to render a capsule of the information that lies in the report as a guide through the report proper.

The Body of the Report

We turn, now, to the report proper. At this point our interest is in the *body* of the report, which all of the preliminary materials have led up to. The main parts of the body of the report are:

1. INTRODUCTION (OR STATEMENT OF THE PROBLEM)
2. REVIEW OF RELATED RESEARCH (OR METHOD AND PROCEDURES OF RESEARCH)
3. ANALYSIS OF DATA
4. CONCLUSIONS
5. RECOMMENDATIONS

Various chapters of the text up to this point have dealt with the problems and solutions connected with each of these parts. We have dealt with the problems of *introducing or stating the problem*—as a means of clarifying what we are researching. We have considered *methods of research*—such as library and field research and the problems of collecting and organizing facts. We have talked about *analyzing* and *interpreting data* or information—which is the next step in research. We have talked about logically arriving at conclusions that come as a result of reasoning from the evidence we have gathered. And, finally, we have talked about the decision-making process and the need to have reports prepared with *recommendations*.

The difference before this stage of our work in the written report is that up to now we have been addressing ourselves to these report processes individually. Now we will encounter them all in one place—*the body of the report*.

Subdivisions of the Body of the Report

The length of the report proper is such that for ease of writing and reading it should be subdivided. The subdivisions are signified by subheadings.

The writer need not feel that he is "overdoing" it by having a number of subheadings and designating even more.

Again, our purpose in writing a report is to create no mysteries, but to create a positive and constructive form with which we can transpose the results of an investigation into a business topic.

Highlighting and Underlining

Although there are variations as to the exact wordings of subtitles that writers of business reports will use, the subtitles are intended to make the content of each section perfectly clear. By approximating the customary subdivision of the body of the report, you help the reader speed along with much more certainty than if you allow him to travel through another undivided "block of grey."

Hence, subdivision headings provide an easy guide to the reader and stress your pattern of exposition. With them you help the reader by allowing him to anticipate the nature of the message you are communicating in each section.

There are arguments for and against the order suggested in our outline of the body of the report. But the point, once again, is that this kind of outline is a familiar one. Whether or not you follow it to the letter is less important than to have a systematic way of pursuing your report.

Closing Section

The concluding section of the long or formal report, as a rule, contains some reference material. The bibliography and the appendix at the close of the report supply the reader with two locations of source material used in the preparation of the report. The bibliography is a guide or list to the original sources from which the report was prepared.

The placement of these materials at the rear of the long report makes them optional reading, available for the reader who wishes to read them and follow the writer's thinking more closely.

Bibliography

The reader can use the bibliography to pursue further for himself the reading of the original reports alluded to in the report.

A bibliography is a complete (or selected) list of the readings or sources used in preparing the report. It lists works by particular authors—or it lists the source materials used or consulted in the preparation of the work. An experienced reader of reports will get a great deal out of the bibliography by merely looking at the references, some of which he may have previously read. You can see, therefore, that one prepares the bibliography for a specific purpose. It is certainly not "busy work."

Your bibliography will also assist others pursuing a similar kind of research project. It will enable them to avoid duplication of comparable research; or if the nature of the research is similar, it will provide valuable leads for them to follow.

To the newcomer to formal research, the bibliography can look forbidding. But he should keep in mind that the secret of a good one lies in trying to make available to the reader the following basic information:

1. NAMES OF AUTHORS
2. TITLES OF ARTICLES
3. TITLES OF BOOKS
4. PUBLISHERS
5. DATES ON WHICH THE ARTICLES, CHAPTERS, OR BOOKS WERE PUBLISHED
6. PAGES ON WHICH THE MATERIAL CAN BE FOUND

Appendix

The appendix is the place in the report in which to supply supplementary matter. It is a flexible part of the report which can be used to make available explanatory material for the reader.

The appendix, like the bibliography, always comes at the close of the report, and it may be divided into two or more parts.

These parts are sometimes noted as—Appendix #1, Appendix #2, or differentiated as Appendix A, Appendix B, and so on.

Some of the materials that may be included in the appendix are: maps, lists, flow charts, data printout-sheets, graphs, and pictures.

In short, any material that would be too wordy, too lengthy, or too much of an imposition on the reader in the body of the report—which the writer feels will be helpful as additional material to the report—may be included in the appendix.

Discretionary Parts of the Formal Report

Beyond the elements defined and commented upon in this section and in the preceding chapter, there are other parts which may, for various reasons, be included in the formal report.

Such additional items may be incorporated into the report because of requirements set down by a supervisor or as company policy. Here is a list of optional parts of the report:

1. LETTER OF AUTHORIZATION
2. TITLE FLY
3. FOREWORD
4. LIST OF ILLUSTRATIONS
5. GLOSSARY
6. INDEX

Rather than additional commentary and explanation, it may be more helpful now to show the reader an illustration of a formal report. See pages 146-157.

Now do Assignment #34 on page 145

(This assignment will be done on separate sheets. Use the space on this page for ideas, notes, or reminders that will be helpful to you in completing this project.)

Instructions: This assignment will deal with the kind of project toward which much of this text has pointed: *the preparation of a formal report.*

The topic of the report should be selected in cooperation with your instructor as a guide and with some class discussion. Select a topic upon which to prepare a long or formal report. Since the formal report is bound to be demanding in time and energy, do not pick a topic merely for the sake of a topic. Be sure, after discussing your ideas with your instructor and classmates, that you have decided upon a topic that will be a fruitful inquiry for you—one which is likely to be satisfying and interesting—and worth the time it will take to prepare the report.

Below are some suggestions as to categories for selecting a topic. The selections are general. It will be up to you, with some preliminary probing of the topic, to narrow it according to available materials.

The suggestions provided here are meant to be helpful and intended to help the student zero in on the topic.

1. **People in Business**

   Unusual, admirable, or reknowned individuals in the business world from whom the student is likely to learn.

2. **Companies and Corporations**

   The pattern, history, or current operation of a company about which research is likely to be found.

3. **Products**

   The working, history, and possibilities of a product.

4. **Vocations in Business**

   Professional or vocational directions about which the student would like to know.

Additional business-oriented topics might include: places, travel, processes, and factories.

After delimiting your topic, be sure to check and review the discussion in the preceding two chapters regarding the cover, the title page, the letter of transmittal, the table of contents, the summary or abstract, the body of the report, the bibliography, and the appendix.

Review the specimens of the various parts of the report as well as the instructional material for proper form in preparing your long report.

For this assignment no worksheets are included in this text. The report should be freshly designed on appropriate materials of the student's own selection. The proper handling of paper, cover, and other points regarding preparation of the report can be further studied with the assistance of the instructor. The student can get handbooks from any library on the typewriting and preparation of reports.

Sample of Formal Report

A STUDY OF COMMUNICATION
WITH THE HOURLY EMPLOYEE AT THE
AUDIO SYSTEMS MANUFACTURING COMPANY

A STUDY OF COMMUNICATION

WITH THE HOURLY EMPLOYEE AT THE

AUDIO SYSTEMS MANUFACTURING COMPANY

Prepared for

Mr. Robert L. Berman, Vice-President
Audio Systems Manufacturing Company
1111 Norwood Road, Wigdin, Massachusetts 23197

Prepared by

John R. Linden, A Communication Consultant
Management Research Associates
2345 Somerset Avenue, Whereon, Massachusetts 01906

MANAGEMENT RESEARCH ASSOCIATIONS
2345 Somerset Avenue
Whereon, Massachusetts 01906

October 19, 19--

Mr. Robert L. Berman
Vice-President of Corporate Affairs
Audio Systems Manufacturing Company
1111 Norwood Road
Wigdin, Massachusetts 23917

Dear Mr. Berman:

I am pleased to send you a copy of the enclosed report, "A Study of Communication with the Hourly Employee at the Audio Systems Manufacturing Company." You authorized this project in your letter to us of September 5, 19--.

The report provides an analysis of communication at your company based on a thorough investigation of the subject. Our report offers a series of conclusions, and sets forth recommendations for the improvement of communication at Audio Systems.

The recommendations should not be viewed as a panacea for the company's communication problems. They are provided as a place to begin. Communication is a dynamic process. And there will need to be a regular assessment of any changes you make at the plant.

We trust that the report will prove to be helpful to all concerned. Please feel free to call on us if we can be of any further help.

Sincerely yours,

John R. Linden
Communication Consultant

TABLE OF CONTENTS

SUMMARY

The Audio Systems Manufacturing Company is a medium-sized company of approximately 100 hourly workers. There exists in the company a communication problem, primarily at the line level. The problem is of concern to the management of the company.

A study of the company revealed that there is little "upward" or "downward" communication. And although there are some helpful and necessary attempts at communication with employees prior to employment, there are few or none after an employee joins the company.

The conclusions of the study are that the position of general plant manager (now open) should be filled or that an officer of the divisional corporation headquarters should take a more active role in running the company. Also, a training program in communication skills for supervisors should be given prompt and serious consideration.

It is recommended that various communication channels be opened—such as monthly newsletters and company luncheons (allowing for exchange of ideas). Ongoing information services regarding company benefits should be implemented, and opportunities for two-way communication between line worker and managers should be developed.

A STUDY OF COMMUNICATION
WITH THE HOURLY EMPLOYEE AT THE
AUDIO SYSTEMS MANUFACTURING COMPANY

I. STATEMENT OF THE PROBLEM

A. History of the Problem

The Audio Systems Manufacturing Company is a division of Calcorp, Incorporated. Audio Systems is a medium-sized company of approximately 100 hourly workers. Audio Systems' principal business is the manufacture of com-ponents for stereo systems.

In the past six years, a communication situation has developed between management and the hourly employee that has become a matter of concern because of its impact on production and morale.

B. Statement of Purpose

The purpose of this report is to investigate the communication problems at the level of the hourly employee at the Audio Systems Manufacturing Company and to recommend changes that could improve communication and, conse-quently, production and morale.

C. Analysis of the Problem

The following are some of the more frequently encountered communication problems turned up in this investigation. They are not intended to be all-inclusive; but these problems appear to be the most serious in terms of their impact on the organization's operation efficiency. And they warrant immediate attention.

1. Little information is communicated "downward" to employees other than that which is job-related.

2. The company makes no effort to encourage "upward" communication from its employees.

3. Few, if any at all, definitive answers are given to employee questions that are not specifically production-related.

4. The company makes no effort whatsoever to improve its supervisors' communication and human relations abilities.

II. RELATED RESEARCH

A review of related research provided a useful background against which to analyze the problems of this study.

Three categories developed by George deMare pertaining to communication proved to be particularly useful in structuring this study: 1) Direct Communica-tion (through personal supervision and management channels); (2) Less Direct (through formal written management channels); and (3) Indirect (through in-formal channels).

Each of these three categories of communication plays a significant role in reaching and influencing those who work in an organization. Each has the capacity to encourage cooperation.

Poor communication or no organized communication in any one of these categories may greatly impede or completely negate desirable effects. Thus, the business leader who wishes to reach employees in an organization would do well to consider these three categories of communication and what they require with more than ordinary care.[1]

III. PROCEDURES USED IN CONDUCTING THE STUDY

The first step, then, was to define the problems in communication that exist at the management-hourly employee level at the Audio Systems Manufacturing Company. This was accomplished through observation and interview.

Interviews were conducted with the union president, the hourly employee's bargaining unit, and several foremen in the company's different departments.

The communication process as it pertains to hourly employees at the Audio Systems Manufacturing Company was broken down into deMare's three categories.

A. Prior to Employment

Directly

1. The prospective employee obtains an application from the receptionist, completes it, and returns it to the receptionist.

2. The prospective employee receives a telephone call from the plant superintendent requesting a screening interview.

3. The superintendent briefs the applicant on job openings, wages, hours, and answers the applicant's questions.

4. If the applicant appears qualified and is interested in a job opening, he is then interviewed by the department's foreman who has the authority to hire the individual.

B. After Employment

Directly

Communication in this category occurs through personal supervision and management channels. Examples are job instruction, work assignment, reprimands, and praise.

Less Directly

Communication in this category occurs through formal written management channels. Examples are bulletin board postings of job openings, company rules, safety information, and general information.

---

[1]George deMare, Communicating for Leadership (New York; The Roland Press Company, 1968), p. 132.

Indirectly

> This communication occurs through that channel commonly referred to as the "grapevine."

The question arises as to whether this communication scheme is effective. The investigation staff concluded that the communication process <u>after employment</u> was not serving the company's best interests.

An in-depth analysis of the problems was conducted to determine the causes. It was concluded that little, if anything at all, could be done about the "grapevine"-type communication.

This left the categories whereby the employee is communicated with both "Directly" and "Less Directly." The communication problems defined in this survey fall into these categories and are caused by problems in the following areas: 1) Organizational Structure; 2) Management Attitude; and 3) Supervisory Skills.

IV. CONCLUSIONS OF THE STUDY

A. Organizational Structure

Many of the organization's communication problems can be explained by looking at the organizational structure itself. Turning to Figure 1, one notes that the position of general manager is presently unoccupied, with the superintendent reporting directly to the division president.

The division president's office is located in another state. He has assumed his present responsibilities by default—through the previous general manager's resignation. Since the company's financial picture is currently satisfactory, he appears to have taken a "hands off" attitude.

Absentee management at Audio Systems has resulted in much in-fighting and dissent at the supervisory level. It is difficult to have good communication unless there is a sound organizational setup. Where lines of accountability are confused, not only authority but also communication is defeated.

B. Management Attitude

The fulfillment of the employee-management communication needs of a company the size of Audio Systems is critical to its continued growth and prosperity. Success in the area of communication requires the commitment of management to communication.

In practice, however, the employees of Audio Systems are not, in many instances, able to receive definite answers to nonproduction-related questions.

The only recourse the employee has is to file a grievance. This results in the expenditure of additional amounts of time by both management and union officials.

This cannot be considered a climate of good human relations. In speaking of human relations, Robert Breth says:

> Human relations and communication are inseparable. You cannot improve human relations without improving communications.[2]

---

[2]Robert D. Breth, <u>Dynamic Management Communications</u> (Reading, Massachusetts: Addison-Wesley Publishing Company, 1969), p. 5.

Organizational Structure

at the Audio Systems Company

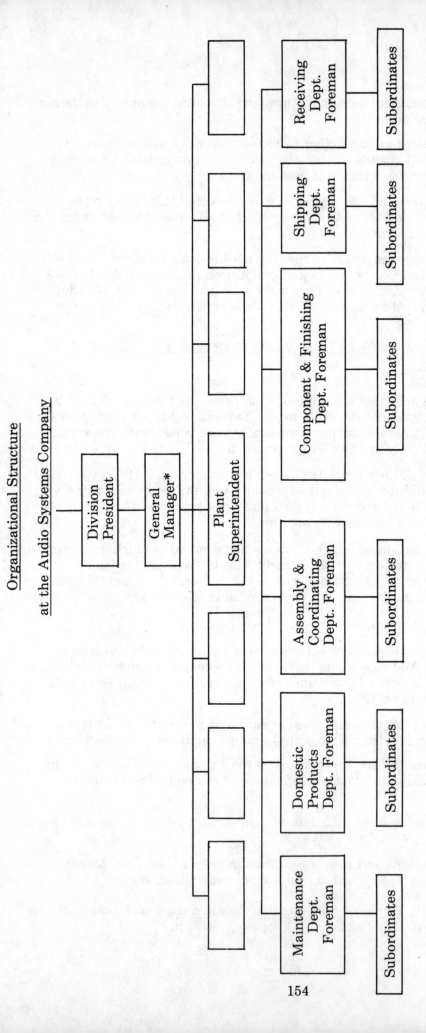

*This position presently unfilled; superintendent reports directly to Division President

Figure 1

The employee gets an impression of the company's attitude toward him from the way it handles his questions. If a "don't care" attitude is exhibited by management, the communication pipeline will dry up; and the employee will either adopt the same attitude or seek employment elsewhere.[3]

C. <u>Supervisory Skills</u>

All of the supervisors employed by Audio Systems have come up through the ranks. No regard has been given to the training of these individuals in the human relations and communication skills that are an important part of their job.

The importance of good "downward" communication between the supervisor and his subordinates is stated by Haire:

> One of the major responsibilities of a leader is the establishment and utilization of a communication system. His communication with his subordinates is the medium through which he directs their efforts. By means of this communication the leader defines the goals of the organization and the sub group; he tells the subordinate what is expected of him, what resources are available, how well he is doing and the like.[4]

Perceptiveness on the part of the supervisor as far as upwards communication is concerned is equally important:

Upward communication performs at least five important functions.

1. It provides management with needed information for decision-making.
2. It helps employees relieve the pressures and frustrations of the work situation.
3. It enhances employees' sense of participation in the enterprise.
4. It serves as a measure of the effectiveness of downward communication.
5. As a bonus, it suggests more rewarding uses of downward communication for the future.[5]

V. RECOMMENDATIONS

The first job of the Audio Systems Company should be to either get the division president to take a more active part in the affairs of the company or immediately put someone in the general manager slot.

Coupled with this should be a straightening out of the disorganized organizational structure. Clear lines of authority, responsibility, and communication should be established and enforced, with the foreman being allowed to make more personnel decisions at his level.

---

[3]See Douglas McGregor, <u>The Human Side of Enterprise</u> (New York: McGraw Hill Book Company, Inc., 1960).

[4]Mason Haire, <u>Psychology in Management</u> (New York: McGraw Hill Book Company, Inc., 1964). pp. 85-86.

[5]William Scholz, <u>Communication in the Business Organization</u> (Englewood Cliffs, New Jersey: Prentice Hall, Inc., 1962), p. 61.

The company must consider and treat its employees as more than just factors of production. The company has an obligation to provide them with information about matters that affect their well-being. Even general information about the company will make employees feel as if they are a part of what is going on. By the same token, the employee's voice must be heard if management is to make rational decisions.

Several steps should be taken that will aid in accomplishing these objectives:

1. A monthly newsletter should be produced by a talented, salaried employee. It would inform the company personnel of new business, activities of members of the company, and bring to the employees' attention items on which the company would like their cooperation.

2. The general manager, or company representative, should hold monthly luncheon meetings with a few randomly-selected hourly employees. These would be "information sessions," with the minutes of the meetings being distributed to all.

3. A salaried employee should be designated to handle all aspects of the insurance and pension plans.

4. An hourly employee representative should be allowed to serve on the company safety committee.

5. An employee suggestion system, with provisions for financial remuneration, should be established.

6. The bulletin boards should be removed from the time clock areas, because of the morning and evening rush, and be placed near the drinking fountains. Glass covers should be added to assure that only approved notices go up, that notices are not removed, and that employee comments are not written on the notices.

Finally, programmed learning materials now available at the company should be made known to all personnel. Both foremen and management personnel should be encouraged to undertake studies to improve their supervisory skills. Provisions should be made for personnel to participate in seminars and conferences which touch on various supervisory skills. And as a demonstration of a commitment to the improvement of communication at Audio Systems, all expenses should be paid for by the company.

BIBLIOGRAPHY

Breth, Robert D.   Dynamic Management Communications. Reading, Massachusetts: Addison-Wesley Publishing Company, 1969.

Connelly, J. Campbell.   A Manager's Guide to Speaking and Listening. New York: American Management Association, Inc., 1967.

Cort, Robert P.   Communicating with Employees. Waterford, Connecticut: Prentice Hall, Inc., 1963.

Davis, Keith.   "The Care and Cultivation of the Corporate Grapevine," Dun's, Vol. 102, No. 1 (July 1973), pp. 45-47.

deMare, George.   Communicating for Leadership. New York: The Roland Press Company, 1968.

Haire, Mason.   Psychology in Management. New York: McGraw Hill Book Company, Inc., 1964.

Maier, Norman R. F.   Psychology in Industrial Organizations. Boston: Houghton Mifflin Company, 1973.

McGregor, Douglas.   The Human Side of Enterprise. New York: McGraw Hill Book Company, Inc., 1960.

Redding, W. Charles and Sandberg, George A.   Business and Industrial Communication. New York: Harper & Row Publishing, 1964.

Scholz, William.   Communication in the Business Organization. Englewood Cliffs, New Jersey; Prentice Hall, Inc., 1962.

CHAPTER 13
PROBLEMS IN WRITING REPORTS

In Chapters Eleven and Twelve, we acquainted ourselves with the problems of putting a report together. This has covered the fundamental problems of organizing a report.

The student who follows the guidance offered thus far will, essentially, have a place for everything and everything will have its place in the report. Beyond this general sense of organization, there are additional problems in writing reports. For instance, there is more to a "beginning" and an "ending" of a formal paper than meets the eye.

Beginnings

There is a difference between a *satisfactory* beginning and an *excellent* beginning. There is a difference between that beginning which is mundane (ordinary) or "everyday stuff" and a beginning which is powerful—one that leads the reader into the report dynamically.

This does not mean that the report must begin with something borrowed from advertising copy—in blaring slogans or statements.

Still a strong beginning is of prime importance. There is a good chance that the beginning of the report *will* be read. Frequently, it is the *only* section of the report that may *actually be read*. As a consequence, an effective beginning has the capacity to encourage the disinterested person to follow through and read the entire report to its ending.

After the First Draft

It is needless to worry about how effective the beginning is in the earlier stages of the report. The writer is advised to put his energy into getting a draft of the entire report completed as early as possible. Once the report has been drafted, the question recurs: "How does one write an effective beginning? What are some criteria for standards by which one can evaluate or measure the effectiveness of a beginning?" Sometimes the beginning written "off the top of the head" may be a good one to keep.

Reordering Your Writing

The creative process may spontaneously generate a good way to start a report. The beginning that the writer came up with the first time around may contain seeds for good ideas. Perhaps some sentence or paragraph early in the report may be the right one to begin with. Minor reordering (rearranging) of sentences or paragraphs may give the writer a good way of beginning the report.

Visualize Your Audience

Visualizing the audience that will read your report is sometimes a helpful tack to take in shaping up the effective beginning. Remember our discussion in

Chapter 6: Your report is written to be read by special people—a supervisor, a manager, an executive, and so on. Read aloud the initial sentences and paragraphs of your report and an instinctive sense of appropriateness may tell you that your beginning is the right one or that it is not.

Three Ways of Beginning

There are some basic ways in which one can begin a formal report. They are: 1) A Statement of Purpose; 2) A Thesis Statement; and 3) An Attention-Getting Statement.

Statement of Purpose

A concise statement of purpose at the beginning of a report is an excellent way to begin. Certainly the first section of the formal report will spell out the aims of the report in considerable detail. However, the purpose of a report explained in a matter of several pages may keep the reader waiting too long. Here is an illustration of a clear statement of purpose from a formal report:

> The purpose of this report is to provide an analysis of the company's current personnel practices.

With such a statement at the beginning, the reader knows exactly what to expect. If he is reasonably interested in the subject he will follow through and read the report. In any case, he will not be guessing about the contents of the report.

Thesis Statement

A thesis statement at the beginning is another way of starting a report. In this case, the writer presents the proposition to be discussed or proved. This is the subject for the paper, and it is made clear in the first sentence or two.

Here is an illustration of a thesis statement for a formal report:

> The current company personnel practices are not as productive as they should be, as indicated by the rising loss of quality management personnel.

Presenting the central idea of the report at the outset enables the reader to grasp what is going to be developed. He does not have to read through much more than the first sentence or two to get the gist of the report.

Attention-Getting Statement

Before defining this kind of statement, the student should understand that taste and moderation should prevail in any kind of opening which is designed to attract attention of the reader.

The attention-getting statement should not be construed to be an advertising gimmick that is adapted to the formal report. This is *definitely not* the case.

Further, where a supervisor or manager has requested and authorized an investigation into a particular subject and is looking forward to the results of the investigation, there is no point in spending time and space in getting his attention. He or she is automatically an interested party.

On the other hand, when the writer has taken the initiative to do an investigation, and for some reason there is question or doubt as to whether the reader of the report will be interested in it, it may be wise to construct a beginning designed to capture the interest of the reader.

There are some basic devices the writer can use to get the reader's interest:

1) The Rhetorical Question

A rhetorical question is not asked for the purpose of getting an immediate answer. It is asked to emphasize a situation and to get the reader thinking.

For example: *"Are you satisfied with the profit picture this year?"*

2) The Quotation

" 'Beware of little expenses; a small leak will sink a great ship,' said Benjamin Franklin, and when one looks at the amount of money spent by this company this past year . . ."

Rhetorical questions, *quotations*, or *dramatic statements* can all be used to get the attention of the reader at the beginning of a report.

Now do Assignment #35 on page 165

Endings

"All's well that ends well," said Shakespeare. But how do we know that a report has ended well? It is sometimes said that endings are more easily written than beginnings. But what is a good ending? How does one know that an ending is good?

For one thing, the reader should know that you are "wrapping it up." He should know that you are concluding your report, not by the fact that there aren't any more words, but by the fact that you have said what needs to be said.

The ending may be directly tied in with a rhetorical question asked at the outset of the report. If you began by raising questions about the volume of sales in your company, you should conclude by relating back to that question. You should end with a brief summary, recapitulation, conclusion, or recommendation that ties in directly with the question asked at the beginning.

The reader should know that you have achieved the purpose which you stated at the outset, and that you have provided the analysis promised in the beginning.

161

Just as it is important to engage the interest of the reader at the beginning of the report, it is important that you demonstrate to him that you have achieved your communication objective. He should finish his reading with a sense of completeness.

Now do Assignment #36 on page 166

Audio-Visual Aids

Television has alerted all of us to the varied possibilities of audio-visual aids. The time in which we live is sometimes called the electronic age. Though you may not use electronic gear, there are a number of simple ways in which the problems, analyses, conclusions, and recommendations you wish to communicate in your report can be supplemented and strengthened through the use of visual aids.

Pictures

It is not a cliché but a simple truth of communication that one picture is worth ten thousand words. Many people in top management today prefer to see pictures, charts, and graphs. They should not be used as substitutes for words and commentaries but as reinforcements or illustrative comments and explanations. A picture of a new gadget or item can be far more persuasive in getting time, money, and cooperation than a verbal description of the same item.

Graphs

Relevant statistics presented in readable fashion can make difficult parts of the report easier to follow. Selected income tax figures set forth in a chart, for example, would make an argument on the inequities of a tax situation much more comprehensible.

Notes on the Use of Audio-Visual Aids

The following are suggestions on the use of audio-visual aids:

1. Audio-visual aids are never a substitute for well-worded commentary; they are "aids" only.

2. Use your audio-visual aids. Be sure to explain any visual aid that is included with your written material.

Graphs and Charts

A graph is a drawn or pictorial representation of quantitative information. The purpose of using a graph is to present facts so that they may be compared and so that they may be more clearly understood.

There are several types of graphs and charts. Here we will define and present illustrations of four kinds: the *line graph*, the *bar graph*, the *pie chart*, and the *organizational chart*.

A line graph is one of the simplest and easiest means by which to display relative quantities.

The line graph is made by joining a series of points with a line. It is used to show the quantity of something from one time to another. The line graph gives a clear picture of progress in sales, production, and other areas of business.

The commonly-used design has the horizontal scale indicating time, and the vertical scale signifying quantity or number.

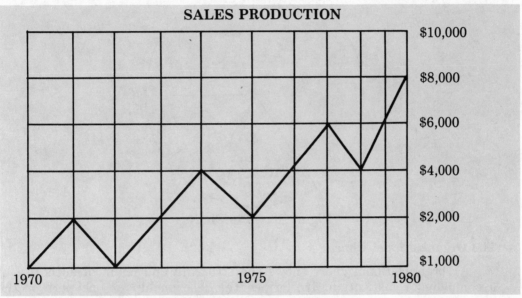

Figure 11.   Line Graph

The Bar Graph

The bar graph is another visual means of communicating comparative data—costs, rates, exports, births, and so on. It uses parallel bars of different lengths to signify the subject under study.

Bar graphs may run horizontally or vertically—across or up and down—and are an excellent means of conveying comparisons of quantity increase and decrease over a period of time.

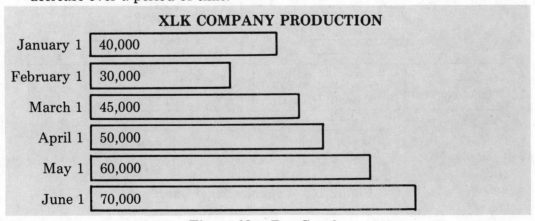

Figure 12.   Bar Graph

163

The Pie Chart

The pie chart, or circle, is used to show the relationship of the parts of something to the whole. The parts are usually presented as wedges, like pieces of a pie. Hence, the use of the term "pie chart."

In the pie chart that follows, the reader can see at a glance how the worker in Hicksville is spending his income.

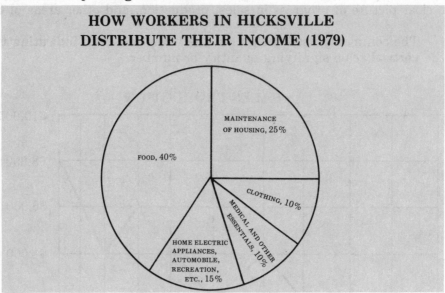

Figure 13. Pie Chart

The Organizational Chart

An organizational chart shows the structure and chain of authority of a company or institution. It clarifies the relationship of one part of the organization to the other parts.

The organizational chart has the weakness of oversimplifying the human relations aspect of working together. It is, nevertheless, a useful means of showing the framework of an organization.

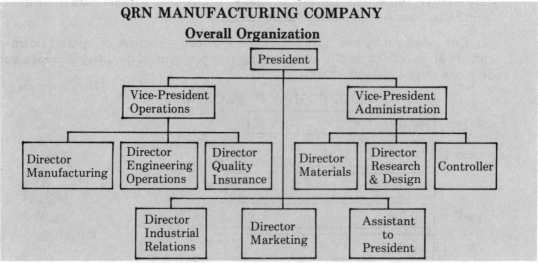

Figure 14.   Organizational Chart

Now do Assignment #37 on page 166

ASSIGNMENT #35

Instructions: Consider the sentences below as possible "beginning statements" to business reports.

In the blanks to the right classify each statement as: *Statement of Purpose, Thesis Statement, Attention-Getting Statement,* or *Vague Statement.*

Think your answer through and be ready to defend your opinion in class.

1.   The purpose of this report is to provide a description of the profit picture of the company's overseas offices.

2.   This report will present an analysis of the conditions which connect the automobile industry's current conditions with that of our company and the steps that need to be taken to improve market conditions.

3.   More than 250,000 people in the regions in which our products have been sold have undergone changes in attitudes that have affected not only their professional time but their leisure time as well; their income, class, and environment are combining to challenge their relationship with our corporation.

4.   The purpose of this report is to analyze the newly-made trade agreement with eastern European countries and the market the agreement opens up for our company's products.

5.   The investigation of this report concludes that an inflationary salary increase should be given to all employees of the company and that the additional expenditure caused the company will more than likely be compensated by increased production.

6.   Is unionization of the ABC Company inevitable?

7.   The purpose of this report is to analyze current pension legislation and the impact it will have on our company's retirement policies.

8.   This report provides an analysis of the employment of women and minorities and a recommendation for the improvement of internal corporate searching for potential managerial talent.

9. There has been some discussion and commentary on the relationship of short-term interest rates which have at times relaxed and at times tightened up in overseas markets which this company has been watching for some time and whether or not those countries whose sagging economies may have a negative reflection when restricted budgetary measures are taken by countries ordinarily cordial to American business interests.

———————————————

10. What are the potential results of an intensive executive development program to the KLR Company?

———————————————

ASSIGNMENT #36

(This assignment will be done on separate sheets. Use the space on this page for ideas, notes, or reminders that will be helpful to you in completing this project.)

Instructions: Using the resources of a library, Xerox or photocopy endings of reports that strike you as being either good or unsatisfactory.

Be able to defend your quality judgment. Be able to specify why you feel the endings are excellent, good, satisfactory, poor, or unsatisfactory.

ASSIGNMENT #37

(This assignment will be done on separate sheets. Use the space on this page for ideas, notes, or reminders that will be helpful to you in completing this project.)

Instructions: Xerox, photocopy, or clip from newspapers or magazines illustrations of 1) a line graph; 2) a bar graph; 3) a pie chart; and 4) an organizational chart.

Study your visual aids and the articles or reports from which they come. Be ready to explain and discuss the visual aids. Be ready to point out why they were used and why they are helpful to the reports in which they appeared.

CHAPTER 14

REPORTS DO NOT HAVE TO BE DULL

Many people assume that business in general, and report writing in particular, *have* to be dull. The term "businesslike" communicates a sense of strict orderliness and seriousness. One cannot deny that foolishness and clowning have no place in a business transaction. Nor would it be conducive to effective business communication if written and oral communication were characterized by tomfoolery.

On the other hand, there is no rule saying that business cannot be enjoyable and, in fact, fun. Effective business communication is neither serious nor humorous. Effective business communication gets the job done. Proof is in the result. Moreover, the result of successful business communication lies in profits or the positive impact of the message.

In the multi-media age in which we live, we are bombarded on radio, and television, or in newspapers and magazines with high-powered commercials. The businessman who mistakenly assumes he must be soft and serious and produce reports that are a block of grey is risking the chance that he will not get the reader's attention.

In keeping with the title of this chapter, the point, therefore, is: *Reports do Not Have To Be Dull.*

In Chapter 13 the problems studied emphasized the need to *begin well* and *end well*—and to provide charts, graphs, and other visual aids which both enliven a report and keep the reader's interest.

Beyond these topics there are additional things that the writer can do to keep his report from being dull. And it *is* important to keep a report from becoming boring.

Someone once said, "The prospect of being pleased tomorrow will never console me for the boredom of today." (*Graffiti* written during a French student revolt, May 1968.)

All of us like a little bit of variety in our lives.

"Nothing is pleasant that is not spiced with variety," said Francis Bacon. Is this an overstatement on the virtue of variety? Perhaps it is. But which of us has not been bored to tears by a letter, report, magazine, or book that we could characterize as dull or monotonous. We know how deadly dullness is in the written material of others. The trick is to avoid it in our own writing.

Using Your Imagination

Einstein once said, "Imagination is more important than knowledge." Exaggeration? Possibly. Certainly Einstein knew that we need knowledge. But he also recognized the great need for the use of the imagination.

Imagination is the process of forming visual images or concepts of what is not actually present to the senses. Imagination, as we ordinarily refer to it, is characterized by originality (being just a bit different from the ordinary). How can one become imaginative? In order to be imaginative with a particular object in mind, you might go through what is called *the creative process*.

Here is a series of steps which will help you take a creative approach to your work:

1. <u>Awareness</u> of the utility of originality and imagination in application to an assignment or project

2. <u>Readiness</u> of materials or data one needs in order to organize a project on a creative basis

3. <u>Development</u> of thoughts that can expand and grow in a relaxed, imaginative attitude

4. <u>Revelance</u> of imaginative break-throughs to the project on which we are working

5. <u>Integration</u> of our imaginative thoughts, ideas, and concepts with the factual and necessary elements of our communication effort

Now do Assignment #38 on page 172

Color and Other Innovation in Paperwork

One of the many things that have been incorporated into the preparation of reports in recent years is the extensive use of color. Color is used to aid eyesight and facilitate speed in reading. Color is sometimes used for the purpose of providing contrast, sometimes merely to hold attention. To enhance the use of color a variety of type faces is used. Variety in size of print and type of paper is also desirable.

Selections of color and special arrangements are based on the various preferences of companies and writers. Some innovation is used in anticipation of emotional response likely to be aroused in the reader.

It should be noted that not *every* element of the report is necessarily "jazzed up." However, more and more are taking on a brighter look. Four-color pictures are being used; unusual pictures and charts are being included, and sometimes samples of the product are enclosed.

The trend away from dull reading is apparent almost everywhere. Interesting photography, where it makes sense and where it is practical without misleading the reader, is becoming a firm part of written reports. Many top executives are so pleased that they are asking for more pictures and fewer words.

Sometimes cost is a prohibitive factor. Yet, there are ingenious ways of providing colorful written reports. Different color papers that do not necessarily demand a greater outlay of money can be used in a report as separator sheets, flyleafs, and in other imaginative ways.

In some cases, colored paper costs the same, or almost the same, as plain white paper. And innovation is important. In a multi-media age, if one does not get the reader's attention in the beginning, he may not get it at all.

It takes time and effort to be imaginative, and it is generally worth what it takes.

Now do Assignment #39 on page 172

Highlight Your Materials

Experienced as well as inexperienced readers are not necessarily likely to want to read each and every word of your report. Very often people read sub-topics or subheadings only, and anything that "hits" the eye. This is one reason why it is important to draw the reader's attention to the various subheadings in the report.

Communicate More With Numbers and Pictures

In keeping with the emphasis in this chapter on highlighting and imagination, the report writer may find that he need not be verbose (wordy and long-winded). He may accomplish more by using numbers and pictures.

Now do Assignment #40 on page 173

Moderation in Innovation

One should not tamper with the truth. The ethical businessman should communicate the truth about a business situation. However, in doing so he need not be dull. This is the premise of this chapter.

The new businessman or business student is advised *not* to go overboard in the matter of variety and imagination. He probably has a good deal more freedom than he supposes.

If your supervisor or manager insists on a strict "block of grey," accept the situation philosophically. Sometimes one has no choice.

However, when it is possible to be creative, use the ideas proposed in this chapter. These ideas are meant to show you some of the multitude of steps one can take to develop and use his imagination by theory and application.

Now do Assignment #41 on page 173

ASSIGNMENT #38

(This assignment will be done on separate sheets. Use the space on this page for ideas, notes, or reminders that will be helpful to you in completing this project.)

Instructions: In order to help you appreciate the extent to which imagination is brought into contemporary reports, you are here asked to do some library research.

The library research assignment is to comb through business reports. Most companies prepare annual reports, advertising materials, pamphlets, and brochures which they then make available to businessmen and to the general public as well.

Your assignment is to Xerox interesting, attention-getting arrangements of basic parts of the report, such as the cover, the table of contents, the summary, selections of the body of the report, and the appendix.

Xerox or photocopy *selectively*. Copy parts of several different reports that are exemplary of a creative type of innovation.

ASSIGNMENT #39

(This assignment will be done on separate sheets. Use the space on this page for ideas, notes, or reminders that will be helpful to you in completing this project.)

Instructions: Prepare the basic parts of a report, *without* actually doing a report, as an exercise in using the imagination. That is, working in colorful patterns, prepare materials for the cover, flyleaf, table of contents, appendix, and supplementary materials for a long or formal report.

Make a collage for parts of your layout. A collage is a technique of composing work of art by pasting on a single surface various materials not normally associated with one another, such as: newspaper clippings, theater tickets, fragments of an envelope, clippings from magazines, and other media.

Use a title of your own choosing or one which you have seen in library research—or in some of the materials provided as specimens earlier in the text. Working in cooperation with your instructor and other students for original ideas, design your own cover, flyleaf, table of contents, and general layout of a report *without actually writing the report*.

ASSIGNMENT #40

(This assignment will be done on separate sheets. Use the space on this page for ideas, notes, or reminders that will be helpful to you in completing this project.)

Instructions: Write a report on a subject of your own choosing in which you communicate solely with pictures, numbers and phrases.

Select a topic with some business or social revelance, and compose the entire report using Xeroxed or clipped-out materials from newspapers and magazines.

This report will differ from the earlier work with collages in that you will go beyond the preliminary parts of the report and will designate the various parts of the body of the report, such as: statement of the problems, review of related research, analysis of data, conclusions and recommendations.

Use appropriate headings and subheadings for each page. Rather than write a commentary use your materials (charts, pictures, graphs, pie and bar charts, and so on) to make your points. Suggest, without writing in precise sentences and commentary, what your meaning is and what the message of your report is all about.

ASSIGNMENT #41

(This assignment will be done on separate sheets. Use the space on this page for ideas, notes, or reminders that will be helpful to you in completing this project.)

Instructions: Select an article in a business magazine that reports on a business situation or condition.

Typewrite or Xerox the report in separate sections. Comb through additional newspapers or magazines, using the ideas expressed and delineated in this chapter for materials which enliven or make the report vivid.

Use moderation so that the truth of what is expressed in the article comes across, but brighten up the report and amplify it by using visual materials. Expand the report by using an appropriate and colorful cover, paper, and other materials.

CHAPTER 15

SAVING TIME IN WRITING REPORTS

What is the value of time? "Life, however short, is made shorter by waste of time." This brief sentence, written by Samuel Johnson, summarizes the constraints we are all under with respect to time.

More frequently quoted is the familiar adage of Benjamin Franklin:

"Remember time is money."

One may regard time as something to be valued for professional pursuits and ultimately money—or for increased use of leisure time and personal value. How one looks at time depends on one's individual taste and judgment. But regardless of *how* we value time, we all put a value on it. As a consequence, those work methods which will give us more time to follow our pursuits, whatever they may be, are worth taking time to study.

Dictation

What is dictation? Dictation is the act of saying words aloud to be recorded by another person or a machine, then to be transcribed or otherwise reproduced. The value of dictation, in time and motion, is that there is a reduction of energy expended by the individual business person.

It is possible to explain the advantage of dictation in simple mathematical terms. An average person writes at a speed of around thirty words a minute—writing longhand with pen or pencil. An average typist can typewrite between fifty and sixty words a minute.

What difference is there in dictation? One can dictate as fast as one can talk. For the average individual this means 125 to 150 words a minute.

To put it another way, one can go about dictating to a skilled stenographer or recording apparatus at three times the rate at which one can do his own transcribing.

Rate of Words Written Longhand	Rate of Words Dictated Aloud
30 words a minute	125-150 words a minute

Dictation To Speed Your Writing

The foregoing discussion should make it clear that dictation does, unquestionably, speed one's writing. Dictation is just another way of communicating one's message via speech to an individual who will reproduce it.

Dictating machines save time beyond that which is saved by working with a stenographer because there is no need to wait for or work with an individual. A dictation machine is available twenty-four hours a day. Obviously, a stenographer cannot be this readily available.

New dictating machines are light in weight. Though some heavier machines are still used in industry, new cassette recorders weigh only a few pounds, and can be carried to work, to the library, or on business trips.

In short, the dictating machine is limited only to the speed at which the individual can talk.

There are sophisticated embellishments on the dictating machine. There are items such as the "Think Tank." With the use of *Think-Tank* (consolidated or centralized) recording equipment supervisors, managers, and executives can dictate through remote control devices and remote telephone hookups.

Some executives are reluctant, or too inhibited because of habit, to make the switch to dictation machines. Dictation machines are certainly not new. They have been around for a number of years. Why are people reluctant to change?

Some people insist on doing their own writing or communicating. Even with the availability of new electronic dictation equipment, many businessmen and students still prefer to work with a real live secretary.

It is not hard to understand why some men want to work with an attractive secretary. Many a supervisor would prefer to work with somebody who is "good company." Be that as it may, attractive or unattractive, a secretary's presence will not guarantee that the work will get done. And the temptation to talk on at length of irrelevant matters rather than the work at hand is a continuing possibility. Socializing is one thing; writing a report in the least amount of time is another.

Cassette or Shorthand

There are now available a great multitude of styles and designs of cassettes. With imported and domestic products on the market, there is a cassette to fit everyone's budget. And the student or businessman who really wants to save time can avail himself or herself of the convenience of taking his or her work anywhere—from the office, to the library, to the classroom. One can work very efficiently with cassette recorders.

The general mobility of cassettes is an obvious advantage. Research materials, memos, reports, or letters can all be dictated on the cassette, mailed or delivered for ready transcription from a cassette player.

Those who are intrigued by working with gadgets and are desirous of developing their executive and supervisory skills will enjoy using cassettes. Others, who for various reasons are inhibited in the presence of gadgets, may falsely assume that they are not mechanically inclined. Perhaps, simply because they need the security of a stenographer or pleasant secretary to work with, they have ignored the numerous advantages of dictating into a recorder.

How to Get Started

The way to inhibit yourself is to get a recorder and simply sit in front of it waiting for ideas to come. This is not the way to work. It takes a certain initiative or drive to start the dictation habit. One cannot do it empty-handed or empty-headed—that is, *without ideas*. One must come *prepared* to dictation sessions.

Two basic steps must be taken to make dictation sessions successful. One should 1) come prepared with materials—data and source books; and 2) come with a sense of organization—a system, a series of steps, a plan, sketch, or draft of the steps you are going to go through during the dictation session.

Preparation prior to dictation does not have to be overly elaborate. However, if one is prepared with both materials and a plan, dictation sessions are likely to get off on the right foot and prove successful for the individual.

Getting Off the Ground

If one follows the steps suggested above, there is every reason to believe that the individual will succeed. The next thing is that the individual should have an appropriate environment to work in. A quiet office or a conference room would be good.

Mainly, the point is to have a place that will allow you to concentrate on the work at hand.

Beyond all this, the rest is psychological—giving oneself a "kick in the pants" is needed to get started. The first dive into a swimming pool, the first swing of a tennis racket, the first swing of a baseball bat—first experiences may or may not be successful, but it takes a certain push or drive for the person to break the inertia and get started. Believe you *can* do it, and you *will*.

Do not Attempt the Impossible

Whether or not you have had experience with dictation, do not expect the impossible. The impossible, in this case, would be a perfect draft of a memo, letter, or report the first time through.

Remember that a perfect draft cannot be achieved by any of us in the ordinary way of writing—longhand or typewriting. There is no magic, necessarily, to the use of electronic equipment.

What we are saying here is that you must be reasonable in your expectations when dictating. You can be assured that you will save time, but you cannot expect miracles. Expect a rough draft of your thoughts after dictation. If you get good copy back from your typist the first time, you have accomplished the unusual.

What will happen, then, is that you will get back a rough draft on which you will have to work with your pen. Rework your copy; edit it. After editing and revising, return your work to your secretary, or rework it yourself.

Just as one would work on one's own draft, this is what must be done with your dictated draft—work towards good language usage, spelling, and so on.

Guidelines to Effective Dictation

1. Dictate at a time and place which is likely to be comfortable for you.

2. Prepare yourself with needed references and sources.

3. Prepare yourself with a plan—outline or notes.

4. Be natural in your manner of dictation, speaking slowly, carefully, and spelling any words, phrases, or terms which might be unfamiliar to the transcriber of your dictation.

5. Minimize distractions by talking without gum or a cigarette in your mouth. Avoid making sounds or otherwise allowing noises to distort the quality of the dictation.

6. Confer with your transcriber regarding spelling, punctuation, underlining, spacing, pagination, or manuscript problems which may be appropriate to whatever you are dictating.

7. Remember, as with final copies of a memo, letter, or report, the responsibility of revision and proofreading lies with you.

Dictation does not relieve you of responsibility. Rather, it makes responsibility easier to handle, if you do it properly.

Now do Assignments #42, #43, and #44 on pages 179, 181, and 183

ASSIGNMENT #42

Instructions: Keeping in mind the guidelines to good dictation outlined in this chapter and using a cassette recorder, dictate a memo on a matter of interest to you, such as some plans you may have regarding: school, family, people, property, travel, amusements, hobby, recreation, job placement, or trip.

The form below is a standard memo form, and you can use this as an outline to your dictation as well. Prepare some preliminary notes on paper as to some points you want to make.

Then, dictate the message into a cassette recorder. Have someone transcribe the message. Edit it, revise it, and after you are satisfied that it is in presentable form, enter it on page 178.

MEMO

TO: **DATE:**

FROM:

SUBJECT:

_____

_____

_____

_____

_____

_____

_____

_____

_____

_____

_____

_____

_____

_____

_____

ASSIGNMENT #43

(This assignment will be done on separate sheets. Use the space on this page for ideas, notes, or reminders that will be helpful to you in completing this project.)

Instructions: Keeping in mind the guidelines to good dictation outlined in this chapter and your experience in Assignment #42, try dictating a report.

Consider some situations where you work (part-time or full-time) at home, or at school. Consider a situation such as one of the following: parking, dining, studying, heating, cleaning, communicating, or some other situation.

Regardless of whether or not you are pleased with the situation, assume for the moment that it could be improved in one way or another.

Before doing any dictating, study the situation very carefully. Make some preliminary notes on the subject and, using your imagination, dictate a series of suggestions which you think would improve the situation. Use the enclosed format to help organize your thinking.

Have someone record your message or transcribe it yourself. Edit it, revise it, and after you are satisfied that it is in presentable form, have it entered or enter it yourself on the form provided below.

TO: _____   **DATE:** _____

FROM: _____

SUBJECT: _____

STATEMENT OF THE PROBLEM: _____

_____

_____

_____

HISTORY OF THE PROBLEM: _____

_____

_____

_____

_____

SUGGESTIONS: _____

_____

_____

ASSIGNMENT #44

Instructions: Keeping in mind the guidelines to good dictation outlined in this chapter and your experiences in Assignments #42 and #43, dictate a report in which you make a recommendation.

Assume that you have been requested to recommend new equipment for your company or school—equipment which would be helpful for the workers or your fellow students. Select an item other than those on which you may have reported elsewhere in this course. Some items might be a typewriter, a calculator, a computer, or a copying machine.

Before doing any dictating, study the situation very carefully. Make some preliminary notes based on your observations and research. Then, using the form below and on page 184 to help organize your thinking, dictate your report.

Have someone record your message or transcribe it yourself. Edit it, revise it, and after you are satisfied that it is in presentable form, have it entered or enter it yourself on the form below.

TO: **DATE:**

FROM:

SUBJECT: _____

_____

1. Recommendation: _____

_____

_____

_____

2. Cost: _____

_____

_____

_____

3. Possible Results: _____

_____

_____

_____

4. Benefits: _____

_____

_____

_____

_____

_____

_____

_____

_____

_____

_____

_____

CHAPTER 16
A PARTING WORD

The student who has worked his way through the preceding fifteen chapters of this book is now better informed about business communications. The guidelines and techniques outlined in this textbook were presented to give the student a better understanding of the contemporary approach to effective report writing.

Of course, this is only part of the picture. The assignments done out of class will have provided as much as or more than the material in the textbook alone. However, it is hoped that the book will remain a useful reference for the student in the future.

This book presents "a beginning" to the student. Alexander Clarke once said, "Let us watch well our beginning, and results will manage themselves." Your conscientious attention to the reading, the assignments, your work with your class and your instructor have helped you make a significant step toward becoming a more dynamic communicator in the business world.

Nothing in the world is perfect. The author of this textbook makes no claim to have given you flawless commentary, suggestions, or materials.

Like many things in life, the work was, in part, what you made of it. In practice, on the job, you will have to be the final judge as to what is good communication and what is a good written report.

Working through the problems of "how" and "why" one communicates with his supervisor and other business associates is instructive both for business and personal growth. Learning and communication are ongoing processes.

Experience is the Best Teacher

Though the student will have some quality judgments in his mind as to what he has accomplished in this course on report writing, the more interesting test of quality really comes later on. On the job, when the student has gained some experience, he may then return to the text for some interesting discoveries. He may find much of his experience will reinforce his understanding of report writing. Then, too, he may find experience has qualified and particularized his agreement with that which has been said in the book. Conversely, on-the-job training may very well lead the student to disagreement, as well. This is all part of living and learning in the real world.

The Future

The future is not going to bring us a more simplified business world. Rather it promises to bring us one that is more complex. With that complexity, communication problems will grow. More and more one's communication skills will be called into play. The individual's capacity to communicate effectively through reports will become more and more a prime source of the individual's ability to succeed.

With his education and knowledge of communication, it is hoped that the individual will see each problem, not as a roadblock, but as an opportunity to put his skill and ability into high gear—*to succeed in business and in life.*

INDEX

A

Administration, 2, 3
Add-On Conference, 9
Analogy, 103, 104-105
Appendix, 144
Appropriateness, 60
Audience: receiver, 60, 76, 159-160
Audio-visual aids, 78, 162

B

Beginnings, 160-161, 176-177
Bibliography, 143
Body Language, 21
Body of Report, 142-143
Business: administration and organization, 2; definition, 1; operation, 3; structure, 2
Businesslike, 169

C

"Carterfone" decision, 9
Cassette, 176
Charts, 162, organizational, 164, pie, 164
Clarity: speech, 21, 46-50
Cliches, 76-77
Coherence, 46-50
Communes, 17
Conciseness, 76
Concluding: reports, 161-162; speech, 21
Consumers, 2
Communication: of ability, 39-40; definition, 5; essentials of business, 46; (... gap), 5; horizontal, 4; of ideas, 37; importance, 3; of information, 38-39; of knowledge, 40; nonverbal, 21; oral, 6, 18; process, 5, 6, 10; telecommunications, 8; vertical, 4; written, 7, 18
Competition: in business, 4, 5
Control and Evaluation, 3
Correctness, 60-65
Cover, 131

D

Data systems, 8
Deduction, 103, 105-106
Defining Problem, 85-86
Dictation, 175-178
Discretionary Parts of the Report, 144

E

Electronic Mail, 8
Emphasis, 47
Endings, 161-162
Evidence, 102-103
Experience, 186

F

Fallacies, 106-107; begging the question, 106-107; equivocation, 106; ignoring the question, 107; non sequitur, 107
Finance, 3, 4
Flyleaf, 131
Form Report, 111, 113-114
Formal Report: elements, 130-139; writing, 142-157
Free Enterprise Systems, 1
Future, 186

G

Goods and Services, 1
Graphs: 162-163; bar, 163; line, 163

H-I

Highlighting, 143, 171
Imagination, 169, 170
Induction, 103-104
Inference, 102
Information: communicating, 38-39; researching, 85-91
Innovation, 170-171
Interactive television, 8
Intercom system, 6
Interconnect industry, 9
Interview, 18, 19-22
Investor or Owner, 2, 3, 4